Transforming the Curriculum

Thinking Outside the Box

Susan L. Schramm

The Scarecrow Press, Inc.
A Scarecrow Education Book
Lanham, Maryland, and London
2002

SCARECROW PRESS, INC.
A Scarecrow Education Book

Published in the United States of America
by Scarecrow Press, Inc.
4720 Boston Way, Lanham, Maryland 20706
www.scarecroweducation.com

4 Pleydell Gardens, Folkestone
Kent CT20 2DN, England

British Library Cataloguing in Publication Information Available

Library of Congress Cataloging-in-Publication Data

Schramm, Susan L.
    Transforming the curriculum : thinking outside the box / Susan L. Schramm.
        p. cm. — (A Scarecrow education book)
    Includes bibliographical references.
    ISBN 0-8108-4177-0 (pbk. : alk. paper)
    1. Education, Secondary–United States–Curricula. 2. Interdisciplinary approach in
education–United States. I. Title.
    LB1628.5 .S39 2002
    373.19'0973–dc21   Library of Congress Control Number: 2001049133

∞™ The paper used in this publication meets the minimum requirements
of American National Standard for Information Sciences—Permanence of Paper for
Printed Library Materials, ANSI/NISO Z39.48-1992.
Manufactured in the United States of America.

To my parents
Jacqueline Story Schramm
and
Ronald David Schramm

Contents

Preface

If secondary schooling is defined as simply the accumulation of bits and pieces of information to be memorized and regurgitated on a standardized test, then we already know how to teach. However, it has become very clear to many secondary educators that to be most *effective* in teaching the diverse group of young people in today's classrooms, they must integrate much of the learning in each academic subject area with the entire curriculum. They must make it meaningful to the lives of the young people, rather than simply teaching subjects in isolation at the same time each day.

The purpose of American education is both social and economic. Not only do high school and college graduates need the content knowledge, intellectual skills, and civic values necessary for fulfilling the duties of citizenship in a participatory democracy, they also need an advanced ability to think critically, communicate effectively, and solve problems creatively to compete in capitalist markets. For higher levels of thinking required by businesses and for learning that is meaningful and enduring, research supports the use of integrated curriculum and instructional techniques that involve young people in social, interactive learning.

At the elementary and middle school levels, integrated curriculum is currently enjoying a resurgence of popularity as teachers seek to make the academic subjects mutually reinforcing and to close the skills and knowledge gap. Secondary school teachers are also becoming aware of the necessity of developing and implementing curriculum. It is also clear that standardized tests based on logical, analytic, and linguistic intelligences often drive secondary curriculum. These traditional assessments, however, cannot measure things such as risk taking, higher-order thinking skills, and creative problem-solving strategies, which are necessary for a vital democratic citizenry in the twenty-first century.

Often, our elected officials, when describing new national, basic educational goals for successful restructuring efforts, use rhetorical devices that stress accountability, rigor, real rewards for success, and real consequences for failure. Subject content is a fixed and ready-made formula to be fed, swallowed, digested, and regurgitated by the student on a standardized test. In fact, many affluent and privileged communities are averse to challenging the old order and ask, "Why fix it if it isn't broken?" After all, some students do very well on the standardized tests that are key to college admission, scholarship, and future employment. Moreover, advocates of the traditional, discipline-centered curriculum point to its many successes.

In *A History of Writing*, Albertine Gaur (1984) reflects on the connections between literacy and information storage. She presents evidence that complex societies develop literacy and mathematics as tools in their social and economic evolution. From the earliest days of Western civilization, humankind has recognized a need to codify and systematize its learning. The first people of the world to create writing and mathematical systems were also leaders in commerce, the first to create libraries and schools, and the first to treat medicine as a science rather than a superstition.

Clearly, the traditional disciplines offer more than a convenient bureaucracy for organizing schools and universities and the concepts by which order is achieved. These disciplines not only store knowledge in useful ways, they also set guidelines for the generation of new knowledge, creating scholarly communities where fresh ideas are proposed, tested, rejected, and accepted. The disciplines bring order to our understanding. They shape our ideas and make life better for many Americans.

So the question is: Why criticize the disciplines if they are in fact so useful? One response has to do with the nature of disciplinary learning itself. Increasingly we—educators, administrators, and other members of the academic community—are finding the disciplines to be barriers rather than administrative or intellectual conveniences. Specialized knowledge alone will not suffice for the present or the future. Given the expansion of technological advances and increased world population, the link between science and society must be made in order for students to make informed decisions and reflect on environmental issues such as nuclear waste disposal, air quality, and endangered water supplies. As a global community, we cannot afford to defer decisions on such matters to the experts simply because they are in a better position to know.

Increasingly, interdisciplinary programs on college campuses are gaining popularity because people are recognizing that ideas for any field are enriched by theories, concepts, and knowledge from other fields. Global problems are not neatly organized according to the scholarly categories. Solutions to problems as diverse as pollution, defense, communications, and health require knowledge and perspectives from a variety of disciplines.

Another response against the dominance of the discipline archetype is pedagogical. Traditionally, curriculum developers have looked at the structures of scholarly knowledge, divided that knowledge into component parts, and presented those parts to students in sequential, hierarchical order. Educators have traditionally taught the sum of parts in order to reach the whole, with the final aim to bring students up to par with adult knowledge and performance.

The emerging state and national standards for science and mathematics are expressed in discipline-free terms. Continued exploration is needed to stimulate the development of a constructive interdisciplinary curriculum that incorporates these standards. To align with these standards, however, we must continue to evolve the integration process, to dissolve content boundaries, and to evaluate student levels of engagement with mathematics, science, and the arts with integrated curriculums. This requires greater responsibility for learning placed on the students, and less guidance in the discovery process by the teachers.

Since integrated curricular units demand a different type of pedagogical practice, they also require alternative assessments. According to Paul DeHart Hurd (1991), "science courses must reflect the ethos of modern science and technology instructional goals should focus on the welfare of individuals and societal needs" (33). This kind of shortcoming is not confined to science. The educational press documents the failures in mathematics education. For example, in "Students Fall Short on 'Extended' Math Questions" (Viadero 1993), students are competent at answering multiple-choice math questions on the National Assessment of Educational Progress, but when faced with story problems or problems that require exploration of mathematical implications, they have a difficult time using the mathematics they know.

Reform is necessary across the curriculum in the arts, social studies, and language arts as well as math and science. Decades ago, June McFee (1970) eloquently explained the place that the arts have in the preservation of society, their democratic basis, and the environment in which we live. Today, in a multicultural society such as ours, research has shown the arts are instrumental in teaching young people their responsibilities as citizens. Yet despite calls for reform, the arts remain marginalized in the secondary school curriculum.

Based on ethnic and cultural diversity, social studies reform calls for changes that permeate all aspects of school life (National Council for the Social Studies 2001). By focusing on cultural differences among individual learners, an integrated social studies curriculum creates total secondary school environments that are consistent with democratic ideals and cultural diversity.

Reform in language arts calls for the interdependency of cognitive and linguistic development. While many agree that students' scores on reading assessments and their classroom performance are not satisfactory, there is little agreement on how to improve students' reading skills and performance. Most secondary teachers were not trained to be reading teachers; rather they were trained to teach literature, which is a different matter. To make matters worse, many secondary teachers work in isolation and do not have the opportunity to share successes or failures with colleagues. According to Ken Goodman (1986), "language learning is easy when it's whole, real, and relevant" (26). In other words, when language arts are integrated with the rest of the curriculum, there is both a personal and a social side to language learning.

My experiences in integrated curriculum have not happened effortlessly. I had the privilege of working with some individuals who not only shared my enthusiasm in exploring this process but also helped me confront several issues and frameworks regarding what constitutes integrated curricular design and what constitutes learning in this inquiry-based format. Although as a high school teacher I had experience integrating the visual arts with other subjects such as math and social studies, it wasn't until I became familiar with the relevant literature on interdisciplinary curriculum that I was able to apply a theoretical framework to the interdisciplinary curricular units I had been involved in designing and implementing. For example, I designed a unit called "Transformation: An Eighth-Grade Multidisciplinary Curriculum" with a team of four doctoral students that integrated the subjects of mathematics, art, science, language arts, and social studies. Before that experience, I had relied on my instincts as a seasoned teacher to design integrated units. Researching the literature motivated me to delve more deeply into this type of teaching to determine the efficacy of an integrated curriculum on the problem-solving and critical-thinking skills of secondary students.

I assumed the role of researcher in integrated curriculum to better understand the perceptions of my students who experienced an integrated art, math, science, and language arts curriculum. I devised ways to more successfully help high school students bridge the gap between their academic classroom experiences by connecting the application of these skills to the world outside the classroom.

My interest in this topic was stirred by Ernest Boyer's (1995a; 1995b) philosophies; Ted Sizer's (1984; 1992; 1996) theories; Elliot Eisner's (1991) focus on the development of aesthetic intelligence and the use of critical methods from the arts in studying and improving educational practice; Susan Drake's (1993) proposed integrated curricular models that mediate processes of change; Edward Clark's (1986) integrated learning model that considers cognitive, affective, physical, and intuitive domains; John Miller's (1988) concept of holistic curriculum that guides body/mind, logical/intuitive thinking, self/environment, and self/self-connections; David Lazear's (1991) and Thomas Armstrong's (2000) different teaching strategies that are based on the eight multiple intelligences described by Howard Gardner: verbal linguistic, logical mathematical, visual spatial, body kinesthetic, musical, interpersonal, intrapersonal; naturalist; and Heidi Jacobs's (1989) suggestion that teachers structure their questions around Bloom's taxonomy (knowledge, comprehension, application, analysis, synthesis, evaluation).

The purpose of this book is to describe how integrated high school curriculum units *connecting* the different single-subject areas of visual art, science, language arts, and mathematics can be used to enable teachers, parents, administrators, and students to make decisions about learning. Chapter 1 (A Sense of Connectedness) offers a framework for designing integrated high school curriculum units of study that includes:

1. a description of integrated curriculum disciplinary structures,
2. techniques for reaching beyond the boundaries of the subject-centered curriculum,
3. equipping students for an unknown future,
4. the world of work, and
5. epistemological questions and historical perspectives.

Chapter 2 (The Art of Interdisciplinary Teaching in the Twenty-first Century) details the following prerequisites for integrating the curriculum:

1. available text sources,
2. necessary leadership,
3. staff development strategies,
4. organizational forms,
5. strategies for organizing people, and
6. alternative assessment strategies.

Chapter 3 (Art-Infused Core Curriculum) includes a discussion of:

1. core commonalties,
2. shifting role of art education,
3. rationale for integrating mathematics and science with the arts, and
4. maintaining the integrity of the arts.

Chapter 4 (A Balanced Inquiry Model of Integrated Secodary Curriculum) includes an interdisciplinary format for secondary teaching and strategies for strategically webbing connections.

Chapter 5 (Two Selected Integrated Activities for Secondary Students) details the sample integrated curriculums that have been classroom tested and are designed to recognize individual differences in students while providing the conditions and experiences by which all students become mathematically, scientifically, and visually literate, and to provide a sanctuary for individual expression. For example, in the "Pop-up Greeting Cards Inquiry," an integrated unit connecting math, visual art, and language arts, students explore paper engineering concepts through a hands-on approach to discovery learning and realistically simulate the die-cutting and design methods used in industry. They also identify the mathematical concepts involved in creating their own pop-up card design and then test them by making a prototype of their card. Mathematically, the students study tessellations, symmetrical patterns, transformational geometric designs, and Mendelbrot fractals. Artistically and historically, they consider the work of M. C. Escher; the art elements of line, shape, color, and value; and the principles of design, including balance, proportion, and rhythm. The second example is "Genetic Robotics Inquiry," in which students explore the chromosome theory of heredity through a hands-on approach to discovery learning. Specifically, they study the rules that govern the passage of genetic information from one generation to the next, and then they translate the genetic codes (DNA) of the chromosomes they "inherit" by making a prototype of a "human" three-dimensional robot using found objects and art supplies. Resourcefulness, problem solving, communication, group interaction, flexibility, and innovativeness are encouraged and valued in the Genetic Robotics Inquiry.

Integrated curriculum not only helps learners perceive connections but also promotes a sense of connectedness and the habit of lifelong learning, which is an essential component of a truly educated person. In the interest of striving to create a better world, schooling must include the ongoing growth and reflection of both students and teachers in a continuous search to a better understanding of how learning is constant and connected.

CHAPTER 1

A Sense of Connectedness

> Most high schools divide their work into "subjects," most commonly titled English, social studies, mathematics, science, foreign language, art, music, and so on. However, the situations that both garner the interest of adolescent learners and provide them with rich intellectual challenge, Horace knows from experience, rarely fall neatly within the boundaries of these traditional subject matters.
>
> —Theodore Sizer, *Horace's Hope*

Sizer's observation awakens us to the importance of recognizing that the traditional, subject-centered high school curriculum may not reflect the human experience very well. Some secondary schools have become more interested in reaching beyond the boundaries of disciplinary studies into an interdisciplinary area of inquiry. Curriculum integration not only connects subject areas in ways that reflect global problems and solutions but may also eventually render obsolete the traditional high school curriculum that features subjects taught in isolation based on textbook knowledge. However, interdisciplinary teaching represents a major departure from past practice; as such, it depends on several factors to be successful, such as cooperation, advance planning, and attention to curricular standards.

An integrated curriculum begins with important, open-ended questions about students' places in society, history, their community, and the ecosystem. Integrated teaching is attuned to natural processes of learning, such as constructing meaning and understanding context, relationships, and concepts within a genuine community of learning. Students' voices are a key factor in the process of developing and implementing integrated curriculum as students increasingly take responsibility and become involved in their own learning.

John Dewey, the great philosopher of the American progressive education movement, realized a century ago we needed a curriculum that created a sense of connectedness for students in order to promote the habits of lifelong learning and an active citizenry for our democratic society. He advocated curricular integration through thematic learning as a way for students to see the relationships between subjects.

Today, the dualistic nature of subject-centered curriculum and child-centered curriculum is still problematic to followers of Dewey. When we make material purely formal and symbolic, we create a lack of motivation in the child because a symbol is only good if it stands to represent something in a child's actual experience. Since the child's reasoning powers are not adequately developed, the subject matter must be viewed as an outgrowth of the present tendencies and activities of the child. This organic need helps the student make a connection.

The world operates as a whole. Units organized around a theme or problem present new information in the context of applications outside of the classroom. When students are taught connections among subject areas, they can better understand that their learning has application to the world outside of the classroom and is not simply a collection of isolated facts. Conversely, when subjects are taught in isolation, the focus often becomes amassing and regurgitating information. An integrated curriculum demands higher-order thinking skills that synthesize material in order to promote long-term understanding and Sizer's habits of the mind, where students go beyond isolated facts to place issues in context.

The traditional curriculum contradicts the way problems are solved in the real world. The traditional, subject-centered curriculum does not reflect the world outside the classroom. Typically, when we are confronted with a compelling problem or puzzling situation, we don't ask which component is mathematics, which component is science, which component is art, and so on. Instead, we formulate or solicit knowledge and skills from a variety of sources that might be useful. School subjects divide and fractionalize the world for students, which in turn leads to their asking questions such as: "Why do we need to know this?" and "Where does this fit?" Almost every teacher has been confronted by students asking "When will we ever use this?" Students are expected to take their teacher's word—that sitting in class will pay off years down the road. However, convincing high school students that the facts and skills they are learning are not only connected but are also representational of the world outside the classroom is difficult within traditional, subject-centered curricular structures.

Integration implies wholeness and unity rather than separation and fragmentation. An interdisciplinary curriculum provides opportunities for students to explore connections between the disciplines and their everyday existence. This sense of connectedness, nurtured by an inter-disciplinary curriculum, enables students to perceive the relevance of education to their everyday lives. This heightened awareness of educa-tional purpose motivates students to become lifelong learners and en-ables them to adapt to the demands of an unknown future.

Connectedness and unity occur when young people confront person-ally meaningful questions and engage in experiences related to those questions—experiences they can integrate into their own system of meanings. Integrating the curriculum requires inquiry into the ques-tions and meanings that young people create rather than contriving con-nections across academically constructed subject boundaries.

Paulo Freire (1983) suggests that students need to decodify or read a situation based on their existential experiences through the interaction with self and world. Genuine learning involves interaction with the en-vironment in such a way that what we experience becomes integrated into our system of meanings. Reading the world precedes reading the word for Freire, and he therefore sees learning to read as one aspect of knowing. It is a creative act. More importantly, the political practices of mobilizing and organizing are necessary for students to transform the world. A critical reading of reality is associated with the Gramscian idea of counterhegemony: Decodifying or reading the hegemonic struc-ture leads to a critical perception of the meaning of culture. If we de-sign curriculum by situating academic study in the immediate context of the students and in the larger context of society, we can enable stu-dents to transform their worlds. In this way, the words used in a liter-acy program would come from the word universe of the people who are learning, expressing their actual language, their anxieties, fears, de-mands, and dreams.

REACHING BEYOND THE BOUNDARIES

Reaching beyond the boundaries of disciplinary studies does not mean that there is absolutely no value to the traditional approach to curricu-lum, which is based on the premise that all intended student learning occurs at the level of discipline-based content. Integration or interdisciplinary work is most valuable if it builds on the knowledge gained through work in the disciplines; hence, that integration is a strategy for teaching cross-curricular connections between the disciplines.

Although the major argument in the controversy surrounding interdisciplinary curriculum is that disciplinary knowledge is fundamentally different from interdisciplinary knowledge, the origins for these beliefs may be found in the differences between the metaphors guiding our understanding of the two concepts. To many educators and administrators, interdisciplinary work implies an energetic state, whereas disciplinary work implies a stationary state. Storage space metaphors such as a body of knowledge suggest that disciplines have boundaries: we perceive that disciplinary knowledge can be limited to specific criteria outlined methodically and often sequentially. Words and phrases like "content," body of knowledge, "structures of knowledge," and "subject matter" are often present in the discourse about the concept of discipline. In contrast, the metaphors for integration elicit images of relevance. Thus, the concepts of discipline are perceived to be in an oppositional dichotomy—that is, discipline implies an ideal place within boundaries and integration implies an ideal place without boundaries. Our personal metaphors must shift also; bodies of knowledge must become more inclusive of other conceptions of understanding since it is becoming increasingly difficult to determine where one body of knowledge ends and the other begins. Interdisciplinary curriculum can help us move beyond rigid conceptions and constructions of knowledge.

EQUIPPING STUDENTS FOR AN UNKNOWN FUTURE

The student characteristics developed through an integrated curriculum, namely a sense of connectedness and habit of lifelong learning, comprise essential components of an active citizen in a democratic society. If society is to grow and flourish in the twenty-first century, it is vital that our young people have an ability to adapt to a transformed future coupled with a sense of community. Few young people are equipped with the skills required for future prosperity, and this educational failure will create a nation divided along lines of social class, race, and gender. Further, disenfranchised citizens may not have a vision of the common good. Integrated curriculum addresses these concerns by requiring all students to pursue educational objectives compatible with adaptability and by fostering the sense of community that is developed through shared goals, cooperation, and teamwork.

Moreover, the adoption of an integrated curriculum provides opportunities to include two levels of student learning, the content (curriculum) and the skills (metacurriculum) (Jacobs 1989). Content-based learning would provide access to important ideas and knowledge, and to the known world of the disciplines, such as mathematics, language arts, science, and visual art. The skills integrated with the content would enable students to develop the capacity to think and learn independently, inclusive of Sizer's habits of the mind.

With knowledge growing at an exponential rate in all areas of study, the skills developed may be the only constant with which to equip our students for an unknown future. Dewey stressed learning by doing, but the doing was to be problem solving rather than repetition of an assigned task. Doing for Dewey was a kind of thinking, and thinking that amounted to anything educationally was a kind of doing—changing an unclear predicament to a line of action by means of a hypothesis, predication of results, and testing. An integrated curricular approach would appear to address these concerns by emphasizing connectedness and unity rather than separation and fragmentation. If students are to adapt to the demands of a transformed future society and share a vision of a common good, they must become lifelong learners and problem solvers willing to assume the responsibilities of active citizenship (Dewey 1916; Reich 1992). In this view, the purposes of schooling are not solely economic but should encompass the need to awaken and educate capacities to learn and grow within all students.

Primary and secondary education should provide each student with a palette of experiences from which to choose the particular colors that their interests, capacities, and life circumstances allow. Such a palette would combine subject content, skills for independent learning, and the ability to solve practical problems. Educational objectives, such as advancing visual and language literacy, mathematical skills, and citizenship, should be pursued by all students throughout their primary and secondary education, although the route to these objectives may vary according to individual aptitudes and interests. An integrated curriculum provides the flexibility necessary to pursue common educational objectives within the context of individual differences. By situating academic study in the immediate context of the students and in the larger context of society, the curriculum allows students to relate what they learn to their own experience. In this way, knowledge assumes an increased importance that enhances mastery. Additionally, learning within an integrated format enables students to acquire understanding through practical activities such as interactions with their peers and the environment.

Understanding the school community for which a curriculum is designed is significant. In *Democracy and Education,* Dewey (1916) wrote, "The scheme of a curriculum must take account of the adaptation of studies to the needs of the existing community life; it must select with the intention of improving the life we live in common so that the future shall be better than the past" (191). *Goals 2000: Educate America Act* (1994) supports the need for teaching students to see patterns and connections among the different facts they learn. In the systemic and ecological worldview of this new century, the purpose of education is to cultivate inquiry, meaningful understanding, and direct personal engagement. Such goals will be vital to the survival of democratic citizenship. Systemic, ecological thinking is increasingly relevant today because of the complexity and speed of social, cultural, and technological change. An integrated curriculum approach enables students to address their world with imagination, creativity, and purpose, rather than making them passive consumers of textbook and media-packaged information.

Anthropologist Margaret Mead summed up the situation when she argued that young people faced futures for which their parents' cultures could not prepare them. Most likely, anyone who has attended a high school or a university in the United States has experienced the constructs and organization of a traditional, subject-centered curriculum, what Beane (1991, 9) describes as "an artifice of life and an obstacle to education that has unity and meaning." However, many people cannot imagine what a really different educational system would look like. Most are not willing to make extensive changes in familiar institutions and habits because of complacency regarding their school, their children, and their community.

Clearly, the traditional, subject-centered curriculum is at odds with the way in which knowledge is exponentially growing and changing in all domains of study. An accurate educational prediction as to what this century will require of our young people in terms of technology, information, and communications is risky. However, many maintain that this new century and new millennium will require educators to prepare young people to be adaptable thinkers, researchers, problem solvers, and most importantly, lifelong learners. To achieve this, we must recognize that the subject areas or disciplines of knowledge at the high school level reflect the higher education curriculum that is constructed by academics for the convenience of advanced study.

Originally derived from the sciences, academic subjects are referred to as having attributes such as an organized body of knowledge, specific methods of inquiry, and a community of scholars who generally agree on the fundamental ideas of their field. But the connections between the disciplines are rarely stressed. For instance, the traditional discipline-centered high school day is carved out into fifty-minute or ninety-minute blocks of science, art, and math. This inefficient and outdated process is one reason why students often find high school irrelevant to their daily life. It is important for educators to help them see more relevance and connectedness to the world outside of the classroom, and this begins with cross-curricular connections.

THE WORLD OF WORK

In June 1991, the U.S. Secretary of Labor formed a commission called the Secretary's Commission on Achieving Necessary Skills (SCANS) to investigate the requirements of today's and tomorrow's workplace and to determine the readiness of our high school students to meet those requirements. Although the purpose of schooling to a progressive educator is clearly more than economic, this national commission's report, *What Work Requires of Schools*, in which they identified five competencies all students should have upon high school graduation, is engaging. For example, SCANS reported that more people lose jobs because of poorly developed competence in these areas than because of a lack of content knowledge. Integrated curricula transcend the traditional scope of fragmented curricula by fusing together disciplines and fostering all five of the SCANS competencies.

Each of the five competencies reflects cooperative problem-solving strategies necessary in the workplace of today's information age. Although SCANS focuses on the workplace, the skills can also help to develop responsible and active democratic citizens. Competency 1 describes how resources such as time, money, materials, facilities, and human resources should be identified, organized, and allocated. For example, through the course of group projects in the integrated school, students should learn to distribute work to group members and provide feedback to one another. Time management is also learned through the world outside of the classroom project planning and allocation of time to components of integrated projects.

Competency 2 describes the interpersonal, or how the student should work with others. Nontraditional cooperative groups enable students to experience participation as a team player. Through this process, students have the opportunity to participate as a member of a team and learn to contribute to the group effort by teaching new skills to others, exercising leadership abilities, and negotiating agreements. Heterogeneous grouping of students allows the opportunity to work with peers of varying abilities and diverse strengths, talents, and interests.

Competency 3 describes how students should work with others to acquire and use information. The ability to acquire and use information is fostered in an integrated curriculum because students seek out information related to various topics and projects, organize and maintain acquired information, interpret and communicate gathered information, and use computers to process information.

Competency 4 describes systems for understanding complex interrelationships. Integrated curriculum in itself is an alternative system designed to improve student performance by establishing the connection between disciplines and, as such, fostering an understanding of interrelationships. Students should not only know how the social, organizational, and technological systems work but they should also be able to work and operate effectively within them. For example, students should learn to monitor and correct the performance of a system and design improved systems by suggesting modifications to existing ones.

Finally, competency 5 describes the importance of working with a variety of technologies. Through the selection of procedures, tools, or equipment, including computers and related technologies, students prepare themselves as they approach group projects for work in this new century.

In order for global problems such as pollution, AIDS, overpopulation, drugs, and poverty to be solved, students are going to have to possess higher-order thinking skills. Although we cannot predict what this new century will bring or what knowledge will be required, many believe that the ability to think critically, engage in research, and solve problems creatively will be necessary to compete in the global economy. SCANS competencies enable students to be independent thinkers, as well as team problem solvers, who will be expected not to wait for answers from superiors. Combined, the competencies also promote the development of higher skill levels. Addressed vis-à-vis an integrated curriculum, the school experience promotes thinking students. "Our future will accept no less" (Erickson 1995, 27).

EPISTEMOLOGICAL QUESTIONS

At the heart of interdisciplinary curricular structures are serious episte-mological questions. Students should study epistemological issues such as: "What is knowledge?" and "How can I best access knowledge?" The possibility of meeting the SCANS competencies—to see patterns, interactions, and relationships, and to experience the power of collabo-rative group process—will not be accomplished through the traditional didactic lecture. Depth of instruction once meant the teacher lecturing to students, relaying mere facts about a single topic. Today, depth of in-struction means teaching higher-level, conceptual thinking by connect-ing ideas across disciplines to extend understanding, foster sound gen-eralizations, and create new knowledge. Interdisciplinary curricula promote the creation of new knowledge as disciplines are fused to-gether in a way that reflects the world outside the classroom. Connect-ing disciplines more sufficiently promotes generalizations and inquiry related to establishing generalizations. Therefore, instruction must go beyond rote memorization drills if students are to be prepared to syn-thesize information and make sense out of the synchronization.

HISTORICAL PERSPECTIVES

Today, we are witnessing a revival of the discussion about integrative and interdisciplinary work in education. The historical evolution of the concept of integrated curriculum provides evidence that educational theorists have long advocated integrated, multidisciplinary educational philosophies and curricula to remedy the fragmentation of separate subject areas, to encourage learning that connects ideas and concepts, and to integrate learning with the five human senses. Throughout the nineteenth and early twentieth centuries, American educators imported much of their curricular theory and pedagogy from Europe, and the concept of integration curriculum received intermittent attention.

For Swiss educator Johann H. Pestalozzi (1746–1827), the highest principle of instruction was the recognition of sense impressions as the absolute foundations of all knowledge. Pestalozzi viewed the young mind as an active mind, engaged in perception, analysis, and general-ization as opposed to rote learning. Pestalozzian theory, with its em-phasis on relating instruction for learning to objects and sensory expe-riences in the real world, to learning by doing, and to the importance of activity as opposed to sitting at a desk, became an important part of progressive educational theory.

Predating Pestalozzi considerably, Johann A. Comenius (1592–1670) was psychologically perceptive enough to argue that the sense of hearing should always be combined with that of sight, and the tongue should be trained in combination with the hand. The subjects that are taught should not be merely taught orally, and thus appealing to the ear alone, but should be pictorially illustrated, thus developing the imagination by the help of the eye. He believed that everything should be presented to the child's senses, and to as many senses as possible, using pictures, models, workshops, music, and other objective means. He also recommended language study and other studies be integrated, as employed in his *Gates of Tongues Unlocked* (1631), a book of Latin and sciences arranged by subjects, with pictures illustrating Latin sentences and vernacular (common speech) translations.

Another great European educational figure whose ideas had a profound influence on nineteenth-century Western educational thinking and integrated curriculum is the German originator of the modern kindergarten, Friedrich Froebel (1782–1852). For him, the Pestalozzian object lesson was a focus for the integrated perceptual units of study of numbers and shapes. Froebel selected objects for study because they had a formal quality that somehow suggested divine unity. For example, the cube, with its regular angularity, and the ball, with its regular curvature, were symbolic of the way nature develops by opposites. Kindergarten activities were accomplished with properties that would identify with the divine spirit and social unity. It required a mystical imagination of no mean order to think of the cube and ball as "gifts" of the divine spirit and to say that play is the highest phase of child development.

German philosopher Johann F. Herbart (1776–1841) stressed that new subject matter must be related to the child's mind or previous learning. Later, during the American progressive era (approximately 1890–1920s), followers of Herbart formed the National Herbart Society and advocated a broad approach to curricular integration by incorporating literature, science, art, music, and social studies. The Herbartian idea of a formally organized daily lesson plan became a fixed feature of American education.

The Herbartian notion of an educational environment of large classes, bolted-down desks, and daily lesson plans did not suit American progressive educator John Dewey (1859–1952), who rejected subject-centered Herbartian curricula based on hierarchical control, order, and discipline. Although he approved of integrating school subjects, Dewey felt the Herbartian notion of organizing them around a central core of literature or history was too artificial. Faced with the challenges of educating a nation of diverse immigrants, Dewey advocated a child-centered approach to curricular integration where the children's experiences (for example, in the home, at play, working on the farm, in the family shop, in the mill, or in the factory) were the "core" that needed to be integrated with school subject matter.

Dewey and other educators of the American progressive education movement, such as Jane Addams, William Heard Kilpatrick, Howard Rugg, Carolyn Pratt, and Lucy Sprague Mitchell, believed in a student-centered pedagogy in which the teacher was seen as a guide rather than taskmaster. Students had some ability to choose their own direction and speed of learning. These educators also supported the scientific study of education, emphasizing the physiological and psychological aspects of learning.

Their work led to a variety of state and national curriculum reform efforts during the early twentieth century, including a strong emphasis on student-centered integrative approaches to education combined with a core curriculum. Dewey and the progressives were concerned with the egalitarian education of immigrants in this country, and they believed that the new role of the school was to serve as an agency providing social services and a community center that would solve the problem of alienation in an urban industrial society. In practice, their methods emphasized student interests, student activity, group work, and cooperation—methods premised on the idea that the school has to serve a new social function in a world of increasing urban life and large corporations.

Some progressive educators also argued that we needed a curriculum that created a sense of connectedness for the new Americans, to promote habits of lifelong learning and an active citizenry for the democratic society. They believed that ideas, values, and social institutions originate in the material circumstances of human life and that ideas, values, and social institutions should change as the needs of society change. The term "pragmatism," which is often associated with this school of philosophy, means in its simplest form that humans should adopt those ideas, values, and institutions that best work in a particular social situation.

Dewey and the progressives believed the disciplines prevented students from seeing the relationships between subjects and advocated curricular integration through themes. Moreover, they believed that schooling was essential to the creation of an egalitarian democratic and community-centered society. Child-centered learning environments were designed to enhance the experience of the child, which pragmatists believed was more important than some outside definition of cultural knowledge. In Dewey's view, traditional schools were isolated from the world of experience. He asked:

> How can history, science, and art be introduced so that they will be of positive value and have real significance in the child's own present experience? How much can be given to the child of the experiences of the world about him that is really worth his while to get: how far first-hand experience with the forces of the world and knowledge of its historical and social growth will enable him to develop the capacity to express himself in a variety of artistic forms? (1934, 25)

In *Creative and Mental Growth*, Viktor Lowenfeld, the famed art educator, aimed to give classroom teachers an understanding of the intimate relationship between growth and creative expression and provided teachers with tools to evaluate creative products in terms of child growth. He promoted integrative experiences in visual arts education and a child-centered philosophy that promoted a locus of control with the child. "In art education integration takes place when the single components which lead to a creative experience become an inseparable whole, one in which no single experience remains an isolated factor" (1947, 20).

After World War II, American schools increasingly became tied to the policy needs of the federal government. The Cold War between the United States and Russia spawned demands for more academic courses in the schools and a greater emphasis on science and mathematics as a means of winning the weapons race with what was then the Soviet Union. A major consequence was increased involvement and power of the federal government over local school systems. President Eisenhower argued that the United States must meet the Soviet threat on its own terms by outmatching specialized research and education.

Clearly, our thinking is often shaped by the economic and political contexts of the time. The move to conceive of curricula in art education from a discipline-designed approach in the 1960s was a political act. Specifically, the pressure for discipline-centered rather than child-centered or society-centered curricula was a response to the school reform movement that gained momentum after World War II. By 1957, the Soviet Union's space program was causing great concern for American national security. The connection between national defense and education was emphasized. At this time, the federal government regarded education as too important to be left to educators. The model for the discipline-centered movement in curricula was taken from mathematics and the sciences. Scholars from various fields determined the content of their disciplines; the status achieved by scientists and mathematicians since the turn of the century has resulted in their exercising power over some political and educational decision makers.

Other disciplinary fields experienced the push toward discipline-based accountability. This was apparent in 1963 when President Kennedy's panel on educational research and development of the President's Science Advisory Committee claimed that curriculum reform, as it had developed in science education, could be applied to education in the arts. It was thought that in order to claim a significant place in the school curricula, art educators needed to join in the move toward creating curriculum based on arts disciplines.

The advent of a discipline-based philosophy shifted the emphasis within the field of curriculum development to a subject-centered view directed by recognized authorities in the field. The emphasis became one of accountability of subject matter within the design of the curricula, and the metaphor of storage space involved more defined disciplinary characteristics than it did perceived connections. Thus, the subject-centered curriculum—where the discipline structure was kept intact with knowledge stored and retrieved—was adopted in America's schools and later reinforced by the infamous Republican-sponsored report *A Nation at Risk: The Imperative for Educational Reform* (U.S. Department of Education 1984). This national report on education, produced by a group organized by President Reagan to examine the problem of education in American society, became an overnight sensation, spurring scores of other state and federal reports on education, and initiating a new wave of school reform based on public advocacy, exhortation, and rhetorical persuasion.

On April 18, 1991, President George Bush released *America 2000: An Education Strategy*. He described a long-range plan to move every community in America forward to achieve the goals. In his speech releasing the report, he outlined the following advancement standards for transforming the nation vis-à-vis the schools:

1. better and more accountable schools,
2. a new generation of American schools,
3. a nation of students continuing to learn throughout their lives,

4. communities where learning can happen, thus challenging every American adult to become a student.

Elaborating on the Bush plan in 1994, President Bill Clinton, along with the governors of the United States, adopted the following seven goals in his *Goals 2000: Educate America Act* that are clearly both admirable and lofty:

- All students will arrive at school ready to learn.
- The nation's high school graduation rate will be at least 90 percent.
- Students will be competent in English, history, geography, foreign languages, and the arts.
- American students will lead the world in math and science.
- All adults will be literate.
- Every school will be free of violence and drugs.
- Improved teacher training and creation of programs in local schools will be achieved by enlisting parental involvement.

Today, President George W. Bush's educational reform initiative, *No Child Left Behind* (U.S. Dept. of Education 2001), focuses on:

1. literacy, mathematics, science, and character education;
2. increased accountability;
3. improving teacher quality;
4. high standards;
5. safe schools;
6. parental involvement;
7. consequences for schools that fail to educate disadvantaged students.

Conspicuous among these are G. W. Bush's embrace of school vouchers and his insistence that schools should be forced to give more standardized tests.

Whether the motivation for federal involvement in the schools is bridging social class differences or winning scientific and technological wars, it is often the teachers and students who get distressed and shifted as a result of the curriculum that gets revised. Other suggested federal remedies were largely systematic, calling for an increase in regulation from central authorities. Many educational scholars and researchers have called attention to the obvious inefficiencies of the basic structure of schools and urged a fresh challenge to the assumptions that shape it.

The belief that how students do in school has significant bearing in the economic well-being of our nation is widely held. Major reform efforts like *A Nation At Risk* (1983), *America 2000* (1991), *Goals 2000: Educate America Act 1994*, and *No Child Left Behind* (2001) are built on assumptions that the state of our economy is influenced by the state of our schools. The marketplace metaphor is the federal approach to school reform and often limits our vision of education to only that which prepares the child for the world of work and that which increases our competitive edge. We look for the panacea that will bring students and schools in line, and in so doing often privilege national goals, national accountability, national standards, national tests, a national report card, and a national curriculum over the needs of students.

Education is about learning how to savor the quality of the educational journey, about inquiry and deliberation. It is about becoming critically minded, intellectually curious, and learning how to frame and pursue your own educational aims. The waves of reforms, task forces, commissions, and legislation have the potential to make a bad situation worse. The mechanical, authoritarian remedies offered by the new reformers cannot solve the current dilemmas of education if they are developed in a routinely undemocratic fashion without teacher, student, parent, and community involvement.

In order to historicize integrated curriculum's current renaissance, Howard Gardner's Multiple Intelligences (MI) theory, which suggests that we all possess multiple intelligences or ways of knowing, must be considered. Gardner, Harvard University's Project Zero director, coined the phrase "multiple intelligences" to describe these multi-knowing capacities (1983b). He believes that intelligence is a multidimensional phenomenon that occurs at multiple levels of our brain/mind/body system. According to contemporary MI theory, there are eight ways by which we know, perceive, learn, and process information. Gardner's early definition of intelligence served to enable students to feel that they all have a place in the world because he affirms the potential value of all forms of learning and knowledge, not simply the verbal, mathematical, and logical forms emphasized in traditional, subject-centered education. Music, form, space, movement, emotions, behavior, and relationships are among the many intelligences a person employs through a lifetime.

Behaviorists such as Jean Piaget, concerned with researching the nature of intelligence, once held that intelligence is the product of a sequential, logic-oriented process. Now, however, many researchers have discovered that intelligence is a function of experience and that the mind operates as a whole, with both hemispheres necessary for pattern seeking. Nothing is learned in isolation, nor do certain ideas always naturally follow from others. The brain is a connection-seeking device, and intelligence results from the active networking and grouping of ideas through long-term learning. Within integrated curriculum approaches, researchers investigate ways to take advantage of these brain discoveries.

CONCLUSION

Today, one can easily see the influence of the university's structure on the high schools and elementary schools of the United States (and most other Western countries). The dominant role of disciplinary learning in our schools is reflected in majors, minors, core requirements, faculties, departments, and publications. Although some are more exacting than others, they are all are organized around some standard assortment of about one hundred disciplines and fields, from art history to zoology. Although high schools may not have departments of art history or zoology, they are categorized around what we in education recognize as the four core subjects: mathematics, science, history, and language arts. These are supplemented by subjects such as art and music, which are often deemed marginal because high schools have not effectively integrated them, valued them, nor financially supported them. The practical or applied disciplines such as home economics, industrial arts, business, and physical education are evidence of additional fragmentation of the disciplinary model of learning. As a result, high school students are confronted with a characteristic curriculum that presents an eternal matrix of facts and skills that are unrelated, incomplete, and disconnected.

As an educational reform movement, interdisciplinary curriculum has received much attention in the recent literature and as such, it is tempting to call this a new approach. However, the underlying concepts and values of interdisciplinary teaching have been implicit from the very beginnings of Western European and American school instruction. From the Greeks to the present, educators have called for teaching and learning that integrate disciplines and fields. There are many examples and models of interdisciplinary learning throughout educational history: the Greek ideal of a sound mind in a sound body; the European inquiry-oriented traditions of Comenius, Pestalozzi, Froebel, Herbart, and Montessori; C. P. Snow's call for bridging the "two cultures" gap between science and humanities; the American progressive education movement of the first half of the twentieth century; the British infant schools of the midcentury; and the open and alternative schools of the second half-century.

This discipline-oriented structure has created a crisis in American schools because students perceive little relevance to schooling and the world outside of the classroom. Many secondary students are physically dropping out, while others drop out mentally, sitting passively in their classrooms waiting to survive the day. The traditional, subject-centered approach to curriculum assumes that all intended student learning occurs at the level of discipline-based content, ignoring or minimizing the child's individual peculiarities, whims, and experiences. Facts are torn away from their original place in experience and rearranged with reference to some general principle. Classification is not a matter of child experience because things do not come to the individual already pigeonholed. The science of the ages requires adults to be objective, analytical, impartial, and logically ordered; for children, emotions are the driving force, and therefore they can only relate to their own personal experiences. Learning is active; it starts from within. An evil of the subject-centered curriculum is a lack of organic connection with what the student has already seen, felt, and loved and the logical classifications she or he is presented with upon entering school.

CHAPTER 2

The Art of Interdisciplinary Teaching in the Twenty-first Century

> It is time we faced the fact that subject areas or disciplines of knowledge around which the curriculum has traditionally been organized are actually territorial spaces carved out by academic scholars for their own purposes. These subject areas contain much that is known, but not all that is or might be. Their boundaries limit our access to broader meanings.
>
> —James Beane, "The Middle School:
> The Natural Home of the Integrated Curriculum"

As an educational reform movement, interdisciplinary curriculum has received much attention in the recent literature and as such, it is tempting to call this a new approach. However, the underlying concepts and values of interdisciplinary teaching have been implicit from the very beginnings of school instruction. From the ancient Greeks to the present, educators have called for teaching and learning that integrates the disciplines. In an effort to make the disciplines mutually reinforcing, many scholars believe secondary school curriculum should be integrated to provide instructional ideas that cut across the disciplines. The focus of this chapter is to review the critical curriculum reform initiatives necessary for successful curriculum integration. Knowledge of these factors will enhance the chances of successful integration at the secondary level.

SOURCES AVAILABLE FOR INTEGRATING CURRICULUM

As the quest for critical curriculum reform initiatives, particularly in the area of curriculum integration, is undertaken in many school districts across the nation, knowledge of factors that enhance their chances of success intensifies. Various factors found in the literature related to human and financial resources, numerous teacher and administrator characteristics, and a number of team-building issues suggest that a combination of factors enhances curricular integration. However, because restructuring how we perceive reality and what constitutes knowledge is involved in the process for planning integrated problem-centered curricula, an awareness of which factors not only enhance the chances for success but also which factors are obstacles to success is an important step to widespread, systemic curriculum reform.

Several sources are available to provide guidance for educators who are interested in developing integrated units of study (Beane 1991; Brooks and Brooks 1993; Clark 1997; Drake 1993; Erickson 1995; Fogarty 1991; Jacobs 1989; Kellough 1996; Lounsbury 1992; Martinello and Cook 2000; Pate, Homestead, and McGinnis 1997; Stoehr and Buckey 1997; Tchudi and Lafer 1996), as well as incorporating multiple intelligences theory in integrated units (Armstrong 2000; Lazear 2000). There is also literature delineating the roles of teachers and administrators in school reform (Page and Page 1994; Patterson 1993; Bredeson 1992) as well as what is necessary for providing a successful organizational climate (Osborne 1993; Fullan 1999). Jacobs's (1989) work is useful for understanding how an integrated curriculum provides the flexibility necessary to pursue common educational objectives within the context of individual differences. According to her, the adoption of an integrated curriculum provides opportunities to include two levels of student learning—the content (curriculum) and the skills (metacurriculum).

The content-based learning would provide access to important ideas and knowledge such as mathematics, science, and art history, whereas the skills-based learning would enable students to develop the capacity to think independently. Curriculum developers should address epistemological questions such as "What is knowledge?" and "How can we best access knowledge?" By articulating shifts in assumptions that underlie each discipline-dissolving process, anxiety and confusion are reduced and clarified for both students and teachers involved in the process. The literature has provided a variety of viewpoints from which to evaluate the factors that contribute to successful curriculum reform.

NECESSARY LEADERSHIP

Since traditional, subject-centered curricular knowledge is structured by boundaries, in order to plan integrated curriculum, boundaries must first be dissolved. Trained as experts in a particular discipline, secondary school teachers can be very territorial, set in their ways, and resistant to change. The paradigm shift required to break down the boundaries and transform the secondary school curriculum from a traditional, subject-centered curriculum to an integrated curriculum can cause stress and anxiety. In addition, numerous external and internal obstacles can result as schools restructure. Therefore, strong, effective leadership is essential to guide and assist in this complex process.

External obstacles to curriculum integration can include school structures such as the school calendar, lack of adequate planning time, lack of resources, staff turnover, parental rejections, and poor leadership. However, resources such as the community and local businesses are an excellent source of support. Parents need to understand the rationale for integrated curriculum as a response to a world that has radically changed since their own school days. Moreover, alternative types of assessment must be investigated since traditional report cards are not the best evaluations for integrated curricula. To achieve these things, effective leadership is mandatory. Leaders who have knowledge about planning processes and who can identify and articulate group patterns by synthesizing the discursive practices of teacher planning groups are essential.

Internal obstacles to curriculum integration, in the form of territorial teachers and teacher anxieties, are also important to consider when planning integrated units. Teachers new to the integrated curricular-planning process will struggle with the conflict of identifying themselves as a subject teacher and their desire to integrate. Many teacher training programs at the university level are now advocating a more generalist approach to schooling. However, seasoned teachers, especially secondary teachers, schooled in the subject-centered specialist tradition must find personal meaning in the new curricular strategy or they will revert back to their old ways.

Stress, frustration, and anxiety are a normal part of the process but one can only be out of alignment for so long. Therefore, resting points should be built into the school year. Good leadership is necessary to help teachers make a smooth transition. A leader who trusts her or his teachers' expertise, provides funding, doesn't show favoritism, arranges the school calendar to facilitate planning and block scheduling, lends a listening ear, provides support and recognition, and is a team and self-esteem builder is instrumental to a successfully integrated school. Most importantly, a good leader makes people feel comfortable and is willing to take responsibility for the final product.

STAFF DEVELOPMENT STRATEGIES

In-service opportunities should be provided as needed and desired by the staff, recognizing that all members involved in an implementation process will adapt to the change at an individual rate and will benefit from different developmental and in-service programs throughout the implementation. It is useful to identify the common problems, which leads to a clearer understanding of what a team can expect when undertaking such an endeavor, and to address the general questions and offer solutions to adapt individual curricular needs to particular school circumstances. Personal contact between all members should be a valued component of any plan and opportunities for such contact should be an especially important part of each week. Such opportunities may include, but should not be limited to, individual consultation, mentoring, collaborative development of project and activities, meetings with students, and open invitations to parents and community members to visit and participate in meetings and classroom activities. Contact with parents and community members should be sought and maintained through informal meetings, progress updates, and newsletters. All members of the learning community should be encouraged to develop ideas for personal contact situations that they find helpful throughout a curricular implementation plan.

Strategies for identifying the special needs of the teachers, students, and the community when planning and implementing innovations are often necessary at the secondary level. If a higher minimum level of teacher competence and confidence in designing and implementing integrated units is to be achieved at the secondary level, then a different approach to professional development is required. Recent research indicates that at least three key factors are important when implementing a new curriculum:

- a realization that various types of actions that support teachers will be required;

- identification of who is responsible for facilitating the changes that teachers will make;
- an understanding on the part of facilitators that change takes a great deal of time and that even under the best circumstances, implementation takes several years.

One example of a published strategy for identifying the special needs of the teachers, students, and community members when planning and implementing school innovations is the Concerns-Based Assessment Model (CBAM), which was developed by researchers at the University of Texas. The instruments developed for CBAM include Levels of Use (Loucks, Newlove, and Hall 1975) and the Innovation Configuration Checklist (Heck, Stiegelbauer, Hall, and Loucks 1981). CBAM is client-centered and is meant to identify the special needs of individual users of an innovation, and to enable the change facilitators to provide interventions to the individuals as needed to minimize innovation-related frustrations. Many strategies such as CBAM are based on Fullan's (1999) assumptions about change. These assumptions include:

1. change is a process, not an event;
2. change is accomplished by individuals;
3. change is a highly personal experience;
4. change involves developmental growth;
5. change is best understood in operational terms; and
6. the focus of facilitation should be on individuals, innovations, and the context.

Strategies such as CBAM are developed to identify and assess teachers' concerns about new programs and about the use of operational definitions of the new programs that they are implementing. Recognizing that successful implementation of a program or innovation is associated with some degree of adaptation, models such as this enable developers and users of an innovation to operationally define the characteristics and behaviors of an innovation and to clarify how much adaptation can be made. Within CBAM, the process of innovation adoption is dialectical in character, involving constituent processes of feeling, action, and choice. Initially, individuals feel a sense of concern related to a specific aspect. Once identified, the concern must be addressed in terms of specific actions aimed at resolution of the concern. Resolution in turn involves conscious choices about further involvement, which in its turn gives rise to new and different concerns.

The purpose of a strategic plan such as CBAM is to assist teachers in carrying out their professional teaching activities as they work toward full implementation of the curriculum in their classrooms. The focus is on the continued development of an environment of trust in which movement toward professionalism is celebrated. All concerned members of a learning culture, including teachers, students, parents, community members, and administrators, should be invited to participate in collaborative efforts associated with an implementation of an integrated curriculum.

Whichever staff development strategy is adopted, the needs of all concerned parties should be supported on an ongoing basis, with emphasis placed on maintaining a learning organization. Clear goals should be collaboratively defined, articulated, and supported, with resources and time to enhance the opportunity for the members of the learning culture to commit to an innovation, thus ensuring appropriate implementation of the curriculum in all classrooms.

ORGANIZATIONAL FORMS

In a world of sound bites, computer bytes, and the Internet, delivery is becoming more and more significant to teachers who want to not only keep their classrooms exciting but also help their students achieve and stay connected. As a result, educators are requesting ways to help students make sense out of the collection of life's experiences and the fragments being taught in the typical detached, overdepartmentalized school curriculum, and administrators are requesting ways to help organize staffing arrangements to be employed with a variety of integrative curriculum designs. There are several organizational forms that may be designed to promote the effective delivery of a core curriculum that focuses directly on the problems, issues, and concerns of students.

Whichever organizational approach is adopted, in an effort to make the disciplines mutually reinforcing, integrated curriculum should be designed to provide instructional ideas that cut across the disciplines. I recommend focusing on the commonalties across disciplines where thinking skills are generic and can be used outside the classroom. I also recommend, when planning the units, regardless of how many teachers and students are involved, surrounding a particular theme and involving semantic webbing strategies within which teachers and students can brainstorm ideas.

In each case, decision making and problem solving on the students' part should involve the same principles regardless of discipline. The focus should be on enabling students to use higher-order competencies, not mere memorization and regurgitation. For example, if the theme is South African culture, research skills, literacy, collaborative learning, storytelling, thinking skills, numeracy, and global education could be surrounded by art, literature, history, science, or geography. This world outside of the classroom focus involves skills such as change management, dealing with ambiguity, perseverance, and confidence. The emphasis is on meaning and relevance through a life-centered approach; that is, knowledge is filtered and situated in a socio-political-historical-economic context that teaches students to be caring citizens in the future. An investigation of South African apartheid, for example, allows for an ethical discussion of forms of social justice in our own democracy.

STRATEGIES FOR ORGANIZING PEOPLE

1. Complete Faculty Plan

Within the complete faculty plan, all or most of the school's faculty agrees to deal with some aspect of an all-school theme or topic for a brief period of time. The faculty may opt to select a new theme each year or each semester. One example of a semester-long theme I observed involved the South American rain forest, in which the students studied not only the scientific and mathematical aspects of the animal and plant life that depend on that special environment but also the ramifications in terms of the ethics and politics of rain forest destruction by humans. This made the topic personally relevant and value laden.

Under this theme, with the entire school faculty involved for an entire semester, endless connections were investigated. For instance, the idea that market forces affect the cutting down of rare hardwood trees in the rain forest connected with the economy and the need to maintain more jobs and produce more wood products. This, in turn, connected with the media, who urge consumers to need and buy particular products made from rare hardwoods. Further, this linked to an inquiry of how eliminating mature trees contributes to the pollution of the environment and the depletion of the ozone layer, which lead to an investigation of health issues, and so on. This interdependent theme enabled the teachers of different subjects to deal with multiple aspects of one theme at the same time.

2. Interdependent Faculty Plan

At the secondary level, however, it can be difficult—if not impossible—for an entire teaching staff to operate under one umbrella theme, such as the rain forest theme described previously. At the high school level, the interdependent faculty plan involving teachers of several different subjects teaching one group of students and correlating their teaching around a particular core such as social studies, math, and science instruction and organized around a theme of interdependence is effective. One such strategy is to offer an integrated course with a new name, such as "Metascience" (for example, an integration of science and the humanities, including art history and the history of science) or "American Culture" (for example, a combination of social studies, art, and music that encourages students to engage in the breadth and depth of experience afforded by the arts as well as the sciences and contextualize the material), thereby combining the content of two or more subjects under one name.

3. Block Schedule Faculty Plan

The third organizational plan makes use of block scheduling and self-contained classes, giving one or two teachers responsibility for instruction in several subjects during an extended segment of time. For example, teachers may teach social studies, art, and language arts during a two-hour block of time; the degree to which the subjects are integrated would vary from teacher to teacher. In this plan, the curriculum design might begin with the students and the society in which they live. Needs, problems, and concerns of a particular group are identified, and skills and subject matter from any pertinent subject are brought in to help students deal with those matters. Staff members may identify a group of student concerns or needs that are typical of the age group and design units of study that engage and are relevant to students. Teachers and students together can develop units of study based on the students' needs and interests. The study should be valuable, achievable, and appropriate for the students' level of maturity, as well as address the school's standardized requirements. The key to developing these units or for adapting a preplanned unit to a particular class is teacher-student planning. The teacher and students jointly decide on specific questions for study, how the unit will be carried out, and how student progress will be evaluated. One such unit I observed involved the historical investigation of student ancestry at a local cemetery. Most of the students in this particular area had relatives dating back four to six generations in the region and the inquiry centered upon the contextualization of the period in which the student's ancestor lived. Students situated the antecedent using biographical research methods and presented their findings in the form of a genealogical chart utilizing mathematics, history, language arts, and science.

ALTERNATIVE ASSESSMENT STRATEGIES

Many theorists of integrated curriculum recommend new approaches to evaluation because standardized tests are not effective in assessing the extent to which students can apply their skills and content knowledge to the world of problem solving outside the classroom. Alternative assessment methods are sometimes described as authentic since their purpose is to determine competence rather than mere acquisition. Assessment of student learning within integrated units of study should employ, wherever possible, performance-based evaluations that emphasize the journey and the process rather than the finished product. For instance, benchmarks of students' growth measure students' performance in descriptive portfolios. Evaluations based on authentic performance rather than on paper-and-pencil examinations remove normative expectations. Flexibility and teamwork, for instance, cannot be measured on a standardized test, but if we ask ourselves if our students can use what they learned in a practical setting and if they can teach others, we begin to promote higher-order competencies and life-role performances that are more authentic.

Alternative assessments can be in the form of a performance test, a set of observations, a set of open-ended questions, an exhibition, a presentation, an interview, or a portfolio. Assessment strategies should be varied to accommodate a variety of learning styles, aptitudes, and interests and should become incorporated with the learning process, not adjunct to its culmination. In *Frames of Mind*, Gardner (1983b) reminds us that we need to go beyond linguistic intelligence and logical-mathematical skills to the artistic, musical, bodily-kinesthetic, interpersonal, and intrapersonal intelligences. It is possible to assess proficiency in the arts, for example, by including written responses that promote both creativity and solid achievement.

Gardner and Harvard University's Arts PROPEL is an arts curriculum that includes thoughtful and systematic written evaluations. Students are given carefully constructed exercises as they produce a work of art that involves production, perception, and reflection. In addition, the students then write a critique of their own work and of each other's work, using agreed-upon standards. Final evaluation stresses both process and finished product. This approach could easily be translated into an integrated curricular format. For practical guidance, Armstrong (2000) and Lazear (2000) have expanded upon Gardner's work by applying the theory of multiple intelligences to classroom practice.

The data used to evaluate students should be gathered from a variety of sources, such as a rich and varied evidence file of progress, also known as a portfolio. Moreover, assessment begins with goals and a clear sense of what each student is expected to accomplish. Having established goals defines the achievement standards as well as the benchmarks, making it possible to periodically track the proficiency of each student.

When assessing student work from an interdisciplinary curriculum unit, alternative assessment strategies are necessary to determine if a student is performing with knowledge instead of merely recalling or recognizing other people's knowledge. Rather than standardized tests, commercial tests, worksheets, or textbook questions, evaluation should be based on that which engages students in challenges that more closely represent what they are likely to face as everyday workers and/or democratic citizens, which is eminently more practical.

There are many ways to compile a portfolio, and three techniques are described here. First, the masterpiece portfolio is a record of learning where the student selects what goes into it. No evaluation takes place; it merely celebrates work a student has done. Second, the portrait portfolio demonstrates various things a student can do, but provides no evaluation according to set criteria. Third, the assessment portfolio includes everything subject to evaluative criteria. In the latter two, material may be collected solely by the student or in collaboration with teacher(s) and/or parent(s). When evaluations are involved, students can help formulate the evaluative criteria and assess their own progress. In this way, they become shareholders in their own destiny.

CONCLUSION

Large numbers of those attending American schools are much too dis-engaged and much too passive in their studies. They fail to delight in the magnificence of the formulations of the sciences and the humanities. They are not "turned-on" by the genius of great minds and great ideas. Many argue that this is because instruction by discipline artificially obscures the naturally interdisciplinary situational contexts that give disciplinary knowledge and procedure its meaning and value. In other words, the isolation of the disciplines in traditional school programs drains the disciplines of their relevance by removing them from the complex and interdisciplinary problems for which they exist.

Integrated curriculum is an alternative that is currently enjoying a renaissance of popularity in the United States because it mirrors connections to the world outside the classroom and better connects with students' natural instincts. As an educational reform movement, interdisciplinary curriculum is capturing the attention of teachers, administrators, government officials, and other members of the educational community because it encompasses the kinds of educational aims that will be necessary in this new century.

If society is to grow and flourish, it is vital that our young people have an ability to adapt to a transformed future, coupled with a sense of community. Interdisciplinarity is a leading candidate for the school reform of the twenty-first century. It is not a cure-all but a direction that is promising because an integrated curriculum would appear to address concerns with adaptability and foster a sense of community through shared goals, cooperation, and teamwork.

Interdisciplinary curriculum can assist in the reinvention of our American high schools by becoming an effective teaching tool for teachers seeking innovative ways to present the material in a meaningful and relevant way. The integrated approach to teaching is positively correlated with increases in student higher-order thinking skills, cooperative learning, and outcome-based performance, and has the potential to be a promising direction for school reform.

CHAPTER 3

Art-Infused Core Curriculum

There are moments in our lives, there are moments in a day, when we seem to see beyond the usual. Such are the moments of our greatest happiness. Such are the moments of our greatest wisdom. If one could but recall his vision by some sort of sign. It was in this hope that the arts were invented. Sign-posts on the way to what may be. Sign-posts toward greater knowledge.

—Robert Henri, *The Art Spirit*

Integrated curriculum not only helps learners perceive connections but also promotes the sense of connectedness and habit of lifelong learning that is an essential characteristic of democratic citizens in a representative republic. It also provides the flexibility necessary to pursue common educational objectives within the context of individual differences. Moreover, it helps learners to go beyond isolated facts, to place issues in context, and to discover the connectedness that is central to the human condition.

Ernest Boyer suggests that we might organize the curriculum not on the basis of disciplines or departments but on core commonalties. He describes core commonalties as "universal experiences that make us human, experiences shared by all cultures on the planet" (Boyer 1995a, 18). He envisions eight commonalties that bind us to one another and suggests that the goals educators seek for all their students should reflect the following:

1. The Life Cycle—Students should reflect sensitively on the mystery of birth and growth and death, to learn about body functions and thus understand the role of choice in wellness.

2. Language—Education for the next century means helping students understand that language in all it forms is a powerful and sacred trust; thus, students must be proficient in the use of symbols to express feelings and ideas.
3. The Arts—To be truly educated means being sensitively responsive to the aesthetic and the universal language of art.
4. Time and Space—Students must have the capacity to place themselves in time and space, to explore their place through geography and astronomy, and to explore their sense of time through history.
5. Groups and Institutions—Students must be asked to think about the groups of which they are members, how they are shaped by those groups, and how they help to shape them in order to be active members of the community.
6. Work—Students should be made aware of the world of work by studying simple economics, different money systems, vocational studies, career planning, how work varies from one culture to another, and completing a work project to gain a respect for craftsmanship.
7. Natural World—Students should explore the ways we are inextricably connected to the natural world by exploring the principles of science, by discovering the shaping power of technology, and by learning that survival on this planet means respecting and preserving the earth we share.
8. Search for Meaning—Students should participate in community service projects in order to search for some larger purpose and to be able to seek meanings for their lives.

According to Boyer, an educated person is one who is guided by beliefs and values and who connects the lessons of the classroom to the realities of life. These core competencies can be accomplished if students are involved in true communities of learning.

Helping students see relationships and patterns and gain understanding beyond the separate academic disciplines requires teachers to examine the practices of integrating the curriculum. When teachers rethink the curriculum and use the disciplines to illuminate larger, more integrated ends, it becomes clear that the process is still evolving and that content boundaries are dissolving.

However curriculum is implemented, trial and error are necessary for educators to acquire the skills necessary to make relevant connections for students to enter a world that is ever in a state of transformation. The structures by which we have traditionally defined education are being reconstructed into new ways of thinking, believing, and behaving.

After educators and students have experienced and internalized the concept of interdisciplinary curriculum, their classrooms take on a new dimension, and they often recognize the intrinsic worth. For teachers, the rewards of integrated units of study include highly stimulating professional experiences that energize their practices, in addition to the challenge of working collaboratively with their colleagues; still, the biggest motivator for a teacher is student satisfaction.

Integrated curriculum is positively correlated with increases in students' higher-order thinking skills, cooperative learning, and outcome-based performances. Interdisciplinary instruction is based on the idea that skills are synergistic. For example, science and visual art–infused curricular units enable students to integrate scientific and artistic processes such as communication skills, problem solving, critical thinking, creativity, and responsiveness to the aesthetic, thus empowering them for future learning.

SHIFTING ROLE OF ART EDUCATION

Secondary students often find schooling irrelevant and disconnected from their daily lives. One way to make the curriculum meaningful to students is to integrate the visual arts with the core curriculum. Not only can the arts be integrated with almost every other subject but allowing the arts to permeate the school day can make students more interested in learning other subjects. Elliot Eisner's vast scholarship and research focuses on the development of aesthetic intelligence and the use of critical methods from the arts in studying and improving educational practice. According to Eisner,

> Artistry is important because teachers who function artistically in the classroom not only provide children with important sources of artistic experience, they also provide a climate that welcomes exploration and risk-taking and cultivates the disposition to play. To be able to play with ideas is to feel free to throw them into new combinations, to experiment, and even to fail. (1994, 162)

The burgeoning interest in interdisciplinary learning offers a crucial opportunity for positioning the arts at the center of school reform.

Early in my career as a high school art teacher, I became dissatisfied with the traditional, subject-centered curriculum and teamed with colleagues to facilitate student discovery by implementing creative problem-solving strategies that made unique connections between the visual arts and subjects such as mathematics, science, and the humanities. As a student of discipline-based art education (DBAE), I began to devise ways that the four DBAE disciplines of art history, art criticism, aesthetics, and art creation could help strengthen other aspects of the curriculum. As an art teacher, perhaps I felt more at liberty to "play," to "explore," and to "innovate" than did my collaborating colleagues who taught mathematics and science, perhaps because they had textbook chapters and proficiency tests to concern themselves with. However, our team approach proved successful because we wanted to find new ways to make our classrooms not only exciting but also relevant and meaningful.

Following Boyer, I am guided by the belief that everything interconnects. I assumed the role of researcher in integrated curriculum, wading deeper into the interconnections so that I could articulate the shifts in assumptions that underlie student perceptions. For instance, often after introducing a group of secondary students to an integrated mathematics and art lesson, the math teacher and I predictably met rolled eyes, groans, and epithets such as "big projects are a nightmare" and "math doesn't have anything to do with art." The consensus seemed apparent: integrated projects were viewed initially as an unwelcome challenge. However, as we observed and listened to students as they worked through the process of problem solving within an integrated format, we realized that the mathematical, scientific, and artistic apparitions faded and were replaced by much clearer understandings. Once the students actually began the integrated project, they went on to solve the problems confidently and with ease; by the end, most could begin to reflect on how beneficial the experience had been. Also noticeable were the students' reactions at the conclusion of the integrated projects. Although many seemed to have forgotten their initial anxieties, their fears and comments were similar to what others who had experienced integrated units said.

I began to wonder whether there were some common aspects that most secondary students who had never participated in an integrated unit of study might expect to experience when undertaking such an endeavor. By listening to the students, could I identify commonalties that would lead to a better understanding of the students' perceptions and expectations of integrated curricula? As a result, could I develop a more effective means of designing and implementing integrated lessons as well as alternative assessment strategies? These questions intrigued me and led me to further explore ways to determine the feelings secondary students have regarding the integrated approach to critical thinking and problem solving.

Remarks by President George Bush regarding *America 2000* (U.S. Department of Education 1991) include the need for an American educational renaissance. In *The Educational Imagination* (1994), Eisner wrote, "Interestingly, how one can have a renaissance without the fine arts is something that is not altogether clear, but the fine arts are nowhere to be found in the 'ambitious national goals' for American schools proposed in America 2000" (3).

Eisner's rebuttal to *America 2000*, the 1990 federally initiated educational reform package designed by the Bush administration to guide the educational destinies of 110,000 schools serving a student population of 46 million students, speaks for many who believe the arts are a quintessential educational component that unites the mind, body, and soul. Moreover, his response alerts us to the importance of the role of the arts in the quest for better American education.

America 2000 was billed as a long-term strategy to help make this land all that it should be—"A nine-year crusade to move us toward the six ambitious national goals that the President and the governors adopted in 1990 to close our skills-and-knowledge gap" (U.S. Department of Education 1991, 7). However, it wasn't until after major lobbying by those who think the arts are an important addition to students' educational lives that the arts were included in what seemed to Eisner (1994) as "a reluctant afterthought" (4).

The national standards for arts education were finalized as part of the Clinton administration's national education legislation outlined in an agenda called the *Goals 2000: Educate America Act*. As an outcome of work done by the Consortium of National Arts Education Associations (music, dance, theater, and visual arts), art education is now part of a larger initiative involving standards set in other academic disciplines: English, math, science, history, geography, civics, and foreign languages.

J. Carter Brown (1993) attributed the nation's resistance to including the arts in the curriculum to a number of factors, including the shortness of the American school day, a Puritan legacy that identifies the arts with "the work of the devil," school boards and parents who seek to train rather than educate, discipline problems, and the inertia of the status quo. However, he cited the Clinton administration's acknowledgment of the value of the arts in education and the Advertising Council's commitment to create $30 million worth of national advertising for the arts and humanities for the National Cultural Alliance as a sign of major improvement.

The education of the next generation must address the whole child. Children should be educated to act creatively and responsibly in a multicultural world. The Smithsonian Institution in Washington, D.C. also launched a three-year integrated curriculum development project that was the catalyst to figure out how we learn.

In *Art As Experience*, Dewey (1934) suggests that the arts should occupy a stable place in the school curriculum and that they should be understood to be an attitude of spirit, a state of mind—one that demands for its satisfaction and fulfilling a shaping of matter to new and more significant form. Dewey wrote, "To feel the meaning of what one is doing and to rejoice in that meaning, to unite in one concurrent fact the unfolding of inner life and the ordered development of material conditions, that is art" (10–11). Additionally, Dewey recognized that the arts had important consequences for stimulating the child's powers of observation and interests. He was fundamentally interested in the ways in which works of art concentrated and enlarged immediate experiences, in the ways in which they moved people to an imaginative ordering and reordering of meanings, to the effecting of connections, to the achieving of continuities. Historically, creative self-expression is closely identified with progressive education, with pragmatic educators who are concerned with breaking the mechanical, the sporadic, the routine, and with those concerned with challenging splits between means and ends.

Arts education must play a critical role in achieving the goals of education reform, particularly in the areas of interdisciplinary learning, multicultural education, assessment, electronic technology, and access and equity. Metaphors shape our assumptions and beliefs about concepts and provide points of departure for the questions we ask about an area of inquiry. Although they can simplify communication among colleagues about educational concepts, metaphors also suggest and advocate certain values while implying foundational relatedness. Therefore, it is often helpful to examine the metaphors we use in our discussions of disciplinary and interdisciplinary work in order to understand the nature of the metaphorical boundaries that guide our work. For example, boundaries are defined and interconnected from some or all of the following positions—philosophy; aesthetics; ethics; cultural; gender, racial, and socioeconomic politics; and morality.

The ways in which personally and socially constructed metaphors shape our assumptions about the nature of knowledge should be a central concern in our deliberations about the meaning and practice of integration. For example, DBAE has a tradition of bodies of knowledge and of individuals involved in arts disciplines led by metaphors. Much of what is considered important knowledge in DBAE is contained within the four disciplines of aesthetics, history, criticism, and studio. However, interdisciplinarians recognize that the basis of knowledge is constantly shifting, rendering the boundaries of each discipline vague rather than fixed. For instance, artists confront or challenge taken-for-granted assumptions about canonical art, historians inquire about revisionist history, and critics and aestheticians reconsider cultural and social biases.

Today, we recognize the ongoing information explosion and the prevalent use of imagery as an integral part of communication that makes the need for arts education abundantly clear. The ever-growing body of information that comes to us through the visual media has created a need for a work force that can interpret imagery and analyze, synthesize, and apply knowledge in creative ways. In addition, today's global marketplace places a premium on the ability to work cooperatively and in harmony with others of diverse cultures. The relationship between arts education, high academic performance, and the skills that businesses seek in employees is an incompatible one. By situating the arts as essential as the traditional disciplines of math and science, we can better prepare young people for the world outside the classroom. For example, integrating the arts enables students to make connections across a broad range of subjects, cultures, and historical eras. Collaborative art experiences, such as mural design or music, theater, and dance performances, develop important social and workplace skills, including creativity and the ability to function both individually and as a team member.

The arts have the power to transform education in important ways; a growing number of impressive benchmarks testifies to a growing recognition of arts education as basic to student development. The U.S. Department of Labor Secretary's Commission on Achieving Necessary Skills (SCANS) report cites the role of arts education in developing key workforce readiness skills; more than thirty state departments of education include the arts in their curriculum frameworks; the arts were included as a basic subject in the National Education Goals and incorporated into the *Goals 2000: Educate America Act* in 1994; and the College Board's Center for Crossdisciplinary Study recognizes the arts as a core element of cross-disciplinary approaches to teaching in all subjects.

The National Standards for Arts Education (part of the *Goals 2000: Educate America Act*) calls for sequenced and comprehensive learning in the four arts disciplines (visual arts, music, dance, and theater) and specifies an array of knowledge and skills required both to create and to learn about the human cultural heritage. In addition to outlining specific competencies in creation, performance, production, history, culture, perception, analysis, criticism, aesthetics, technology, and appreciation, the standards call for students to be able to relate various types of arts knowledge and skills within and across the arts disciplines. National education in the arts has been placed on our national agenda; for those of us who have long advocated the centrality of the arts in the education of all students, this is an opportunity and a challenge. However, this is not to say that concerns and apprehensions do not surround the standardization of instruction in the arts because the visual arts encompass differing forms and styles.

Creating visual forms involves a wide variety of tools, techniques, and processes. In the spring of 1994, the National Art Education Association (NAEA) published the *National Standards for Visual Arts Education*, in which Jerome Hausman (1994) urged art educators to actively support the *Goals 2000: Educate America Act*. "The hope being expressed is that the standards we establish will be responsive to the nature of artistic processes as well as the qualitative dimensions involved in making critical judgments and developing historical insights" (1). Currently, the arts standards are voluntary and are not a federal mandate for schools, although there is evidence that this is changing. At the time of this writing, school districts are free to choose how to use the standards, and adopting the standards does not require the adoption of a single curriculum with prescribed teaching methods or materials. However, the standards clearly state that a comprehensive structured program in the visual arts is an essential part of the education of every American student and that when states and school districts adopt the standards, they will be taking a stand for rigor and discipline in arts instruction.

RATIONALE FOR INTEGRATING THE CURRICULUM

With knowledge constantly growing and changing in all areas of study, we in education cannot adequately predict what this new century nor this new millennium will demand of our students. The age of technology, information, and communications rewards those nations whose people learn new skills to stay ahead; in short, we live in a world that rewards learning. Therefore, it is important for educators to prepare young people to be adaptable thinkers, researchers, problem solvers, and most importantly, lifelong learners. To achieve this, we must recognize that the subject areas or disciplines of knowledge around which the curriculum has traditionally been organized are, as Beane (1991) argues, arbitrarily defined territories carved out by academics for the convenience of advanced study.

These disciplines contain much of what is known, but their boundaries serve to fractionalize knowledge into artificial components, thus limiting our ingenuity. In the world outside the classroom, problems are not solved in fifty-five-minute time blocks of history, art, and science. Rather, data is gathered from all our resources to generate solutions that are essentially multidisciplinary in nature. Thus, the traditional curriculum does not reflect the social reality that our students experience in their everyday lives.

Jacobs (1991) suggests that the discipline-oriented structure of traditional curricula has created a crisis in American schools. In a nationwide study—probing the views of over 1,300 American teenagers (Black, White and Hispanic) in grades nine through twelve, in both private and public schools—the researchers suggest that many of today's students are dropping out mentally, sitting passively in their classrooms waiting to survive the day (Johnson, Farkas, and Bers 1997). Although the causes of early school leaving rates are complex, the traditional discipline structure may be a contributing factor. An integrated curriculum provides opportunities for students to explore connections between the disciplines and their everyday existence. It also enables learners to perceive connections between the disciplines. The sense of connectedness nurtured by an integrated curriculum enables students to perceive the relevance of education outside the classroom. This heightened awareness of educational purpose may also motivate students to become lifelong learners, essential in a contemporary citizen, enabling them to adapt to the demands of an unknown future.

RATIONALE FOR INTEGRATING MATHEMATICS
AND SCIENCE WITH THE ARTS

To ensure math and science requirements are covered, the best route to integrating curriculum is through the sciences. Many schools emphasize using the arts to demonstrate understanding of the learning. For example, the potential for teaching the arts in science has been well developed by Waldorf schools who advocate learning as a cooperative venture where the creative and artistic are emphasized. In this approach, the power of imagination is important in learning, and activities are designed so that content is connected to the student's experience. However, a problem with the arts in science approach is differentiating between content and strategy. In order for the arts not to be extorted, it is important to work hard to achieve the proper balance of science and art without shortchanging either.

MAINTAINING THE INTEGRITY OF THE ARTS

The arts are often used in integrated language arts and social studies lessons, especially at the elementary and middle school levels. When it comes to math and science integrated units at the high school level, it is particularly important to work to make sure the arts are not shortchanged. If they become simply a handmaiden to enrich subjects like math and science or are used as the sugar-coating to make the math and science pills easier to swallow, the intrinsic value of the arts will be diminished, and authentic arts goals will not be met.

It is good to be cautious and apprehensive about changes such as curricular designs that present the arts as only aids to instruction in other disciplines. With the perpetual bandwagon of educational reforms, integrated units of study at the high school level might appear to be trendy and transient to veteran teachers who believe they have seen it all before. However, if educators and curriculum designers are careful to maintain the integrity of the arts, the most important goal of integrating the curriculum can be reached, enabling students to make connections between concepts and across subjects.

CHAPTER 4

Evolution of a Balanced Inquiry Model of Integrated Secondary Curriculum vis-à-vis the Genetic Robotics Unit

> Art is a quality of doing and of what is done. Only outwardly, then, can it be designated by a noun substantive. Since it adheres to the manner and content of doing, it is adjectival in nature.
>
> —John Dewey, *Art As Experience*

Secondary school curriculums are subject-centered to reflect the traditional fields of study in institutions of higher education, standardized college entrance exams, and increasingly mandated national and state accountability standards. However, in a world of sound bites, computer bytes, and the Internet, delivery is becoming increasingly significant to teachers who want to not only keep their classrooms exciting but also help their students achieve. As a result, educators are requesting ways to help students make sense out of the collection of life's experiences and the fragments being taught in the typical detached, overdepartmentalized school curriculum, and administrators are requesting ways to help organize staffing arrangements to be employed with block scheduling and a variety of integrative curriculum designs.

The Balanced Inquiry Model of interdisciplinary teaching represents a major departure from traditional practices at the high school level because it calls for juxtaposing and making cross-curricular connections between the content and skills of both the "academic" subjects such as mathematics, science, and language arts, and the "elective or nonacademic" subjects of art, music, drama, and physical education. In other words, "balancing" the arts and sciences by uniting the right brain and the left brain.

The Balanced Inquiry Model is based on the following assumptions:

1. The curriculum should be designed to provide instructional ideas that cut across all disciplines.
2. Artificial boundaries have traditionally been set up between the disciplines.
3. There is a hierarchy of importance assigned to the disciplines, with the sciences at the top and the arts at the bottom.
4. Throughout their school careers, students internalize these hierarchies and boundaries as fixed.
5. Enabling students to find workable solutions to shift those hierarchies and boundaries is critical for cross-curricular connections.

The Balanced Inquiry Model views the curriculum through the lens of praxis that integrates content from two or more discreet disciplines to increase the relevance of an overarching theme that incorporates the whole. Moreover, the model is based on the following goals:

- student as critical thinker;
- student as creative problem solver;
- student as active, independent learner;
- student proficient in the use of symbols to express feelings/ideas;
- student as responsive to the aesthetic;
- student capable of placing him/herself in time and space;
- student as researcher;
- student as aware of the world of work.

MY EARLY EXPERIENCES INTEGRATING ART AND MATH

While teaching in an area of Greater Cincinnati comprised of working-class poor and middle-class families, I had the great fortune of working with a twenty-year mathematics veteran who shared my teaching philosophy of student as self-directed learner. We were both unsatisfied with the traditional, isolated, subject-centered high school classroom and interested in bridging the gap between mathematics and art. Over a four-year period, the math teacher and I teamed to facilitate student discovery by implementing creative problem-solving strategies that made unique connections between the traditional subjects of mathematics (geometry) and visual art. Our team approach, which often included foreign language, English, and social studies teachers, proved successful because we were desirous of continuing to make our secondary classrooms not only exciting but also relevant and meaningful (Schramm 1996b).

Although less than 20 percent of the student body at this particular school attended a four-year postsecondary institution upon graduation from high school, we had almost universal parental support in the community for our integrated curricular ideas. However, our efforts were not without obstacles, which often included time constraints (we did not have the benefit of block scheduling at this school), a lack of administrative support (the principal often undermined our efforts by refusing to grant us joint planning time), and student insecurity (the students sometimes felt uncomfortable combining math and art because they were used to a more traditional, segregated approach to different subjects).

EVOLUTION OF THE BALANCED INQUIRY MODEL

Interestingly, although the parents were actively involved in their children's educational welfare, my experiences in another Greater Cincinnati high school that was located in a more economically advantaged community contrasted greatly with the poorer community. The group of economically advantaged parents and students deemed their existing traditional, subject-centered high school with its "core" curriculum of mathematics, science, language arts, and social studies, and its "encore" of music and visual art at the highest degree of scholastic rank since students scored so well on state proficiency tests and other standardized exams. Almost all students went on to attend a four-year postsecondary institution and therefore, this privileged community was understandably skeptical and suspicious of any curricular modifications that were not specifically in line with standardized tests and college entrance exams.

Moreover, their focus on the established formula of the subject-centered curricular structures led to an almost universally undisputed acceptance of the established educational practices instead of the type of risk taking that advances expansion and growth. The arts were seen as an "encore" to the "core" of an academic class such as biology, and many in the community did not perceive any connection between art and science. For instance, one mother of a male art student in the eleventh grade wrote, "Whatever happened to the time when art was about drawing, painting, and learning about different artists and techniques?" Clearly, this particular parent was referring to her high school experiences in art class and expected that her son's experiences be identical to her own. Moreover, the implication was that the arts are not worthy of any time outside of class and in place solely to provide a "break" from the rigors of "academic" classes.

I began to think about ways to link the theory on integrated curriculum design and implementation with high school experiences. Since most scholars focused on the elementary and middle school levels, I found a secondary model in need of development. Interdisciplinary teaching at the high school level represented a major departure from the practices of this school, so I had to ensure that my curriculum team's efforts to blend the subjects of art and science successfully accounted for the science content that the graded course of study dictated we teach relative to the biological science of genetics. In order to do this and simultaneously make art and science reciprocally empowered, I developed an integrated curricular prototype specifically for this school that I called the Balanced Inquiry Model (Schramm 1999a). Because this model requires juxtaposing and making cross-curricular connections between the content of two or more subjects, I suggested that our new integrated course be given a new name. Therefore, the combined classes of Biology I and Art I were consolidated and renamed "Genetic Robotics: A Three-Dimensional Scientific Inquiry."

The view of the learner who constructs meaning and advocates using real-life problems with more than one right answer was promoted in the Balanced Inquiry Model of interdisciplinary curriculum. Therefore, the evaluation was based on alternative assessment strategies rather than on standardized examinations because our primary purpose was to determine competence rather than mere acquisition. For example, we asked: Can our students use what they've learned in a pragmatic setting? Can they teach others? Can they transfer what they have learned to other situations?

After reviewing the literature, I realized I needed to provide some intellectual and practical criteria for successful curriculum integration to satisfy this community. I began to articulate the need for integrated thinking and learning skills across the curriculum and the usefulness of thematic learning by providing the wisdom of the versatility that is so very necessary to pursue common educational objectives within the context of individual differences.

Specifically, the curricular content provided access to important ideas and knowledge, such as the mathematics involved in the statistical analysis of genetic prediction, the basic biological science involved in learning about human genetic inheritance, and the history of science and art. The metacurricular skills-based learning enabled students to develop the capacity to think independently and creatively solve problems by creating a three-dimensional robotic sculpture.

For the practical "nuts and bolts" required to make this unit adaptable to the high school level, the teaching team and I identified some of the common problems we might encounter. This led us to a clearer understanding of what we might expect throughout the implementation of the unit. Together, we addressed general questions and offered solutions to adapt individual curricular needs to particular school circumstances. It was agreed that our interdisciplinary team of teachers representing the different subjects of biology, art, and language arts would team teach the group of students. Teachers would take turns being the "lead" teacher depending on when necessary specialized information was addressed.

Our curriculum design began with the students and the society in which they live. The teaching team and I adapted the unit to the particular students we had in class, which was a very important point in a privileged community like this one, where some parents and students are skeptical of exploring any curricular modifications such as integrated curriculum. We identified the requirements, questions, and concerns of our particular group of parents and students and identified the skills and subject matter from language arts and biology. For example, we first identified a group of student needs and next we designed the "Genetic Robotics" unit to engage and be relevant to our students (Schramm, 2000).

The teachers identified their subject areas and their specialties and taught within that framework. We first decided that our unit would focus on the particular theme "pioneers," then we began brainstorming ideas, and subsequently clustered and reclustered our ideas into a semantic web. Semantic webbing is a useful tool for discovering natural and obvious connections. For example, the strength of the disciplines of art (Nam June Paik and his pioneering of video technology) and of biology (Gregor Mendel and his pioneering of genetics through pea-pod experiments) were kept intact while providing a connection between the two diverse fields of knowledge.

As we brainstormed, one person would write on a large piece of newsprint paper with a marker so we could flip back to our ideas and refine them as we went along. For example, our interdisciplinary approach to integrated curricula focused on the commonalties across disciplines where thinking skills are generic and could be used outside the classroom. We asked ourselves, "How can we teach our students higher-order thinking skills?"

Because learning transcends the discipline boundaries and because higher-order thinking skills are viewed as universal, we planned the "pioneering" unit so that the decision making and problem solving on both the art and the science students' part involved the same principles. For example, they learned important literacy skills such as library research, including the Modern Language Association (MLA) style format; collaborative learning skills; reflective journalizing skills; thinking skills; numeracy skills, including decision matrices and Punnett square statistical calculations; and global educational issues such as the ethics surrounding the cloning debate.

The idea that we should teach students to be productive citizens in the future was a focus of ours as well and involved taking the students to a state-of-the-art genetic laboratory and an artist's studio to help them link meaning and relevance by filtering their knowledge through a real-world context. In addition, they addressed the contemporary issue of biological ethics in reflective journal entries on the cloning debate, which helped them to synthesize a type of conscientious and humane circumstance often required of responsible democratic citizens.

Our specific interdisciplinary curriculum took into consideration students of all abilities and learning styles and was designed to reinforce the biological science of genetics (DNA) in conjunction with the principles and elements of three-dimensional visual art (sculpture). We felt a responsibility to provide the best possible conditions for learning and opportunities for every learner to participate. Therefore, our curriculum included a hands-on activity, with specific criteria to explain its basis, its organization, its expectations, and its method, and emphases on portfolio development.

APPLICATIONS OF SCIENCE
AND ART OUTSIDE THE CLASSROOM

Applications of science and art outside of the classroom were supported by a field trip designed to familiarize the students with the work of molecular geneticist Tom Doetschman at the University of Cincinnati Medical Center and the sculpture of sculptor Nam June Paik at the Michael Solway Gallery, the Cincinnati Art Museum (CAM), and the Contemporary Art Center (CAC). In the morning, Dr. Doetschman, who uses advanced genetic technology to breed special strains of mice for medical research, gave a presentation to the students in the state-of-the-art lecture room at the center and took them on a guided tour of the laboratories.

In the afternoon, the students visited the studio of Nam June Paik, the internationally known Korean artist whose work incorporates video technology and sculpture. Students witnessed firsthand the construction involved in Paik's finished works. The gallery owner, Michael Solway, gave the students a personalized tour of the facility and discussed the work of Paik with them. The students also had the opportunity to view Paik's masterpiece, *Powell Crosley Jr.,* which is a sculpture based on the historical memorabilia of radio and television pioneer, inventor, engineer, scientist, and native Cincinnatian Powell Crosley, at the CAM and *Metrobot,* a monumental outdoor public robotic sculpture equipped with a digital display designed to advertise exhibits at the CAC. Students wrote reaction papers to the field trip and overall seemed to begin to make a connection between the arts and sciences from the experience. According to one ninth-grader, "The robot I saw by Nam June Paik was pretty cool because you would have to know a lot of science stuff to build one, or be a skilled electrician or engineer." Another student wrote, "At the U.C. Medical Center I got several creative ideas for my project. The scientists are creative in the ways they manipulate genes and alter them to learn about certain inherited diseases."

A visiting local artist and sculptor, Fred Ellenberger, also spoke to the students about the relationship between science and art. He explained the basic principles involved in constructing sculptures and the necessity of incorporating the talents of a variety of scientific engineers, including mechanics, designers, physicists, and technicians.

We felt the field trip and the speaker would help capture the attention of the students. The field trips, projects, movies, and guest speakers made the biology more interesting and raised social awareness. As the students learned how biology affects their lives, they were given the incentive and perhaps were empowered to act, which stimulates the process of asking questions, the first step of the scientific method.

In an effort to make the two subjects mutually reinforcing, this interdisciplinary curriculum was designed to provide instructional ideas that cut across the subjects of science and art. The aim of this unit was to provide all students with access to experiences that would allow them to go beyond isolated facts to put issues in context. We planned and created a learning situation that not only accommodated the individual aptitudes, interests, and learning styles of our students but also promoted student discovery using creative problem-solving strategies between the traditional subjects of biology and art. In an effort to make the two subjects mutually reinforcing, our secondary school integrated curriculum was designed to provide instructional ideas that cut across the disciplines.

We enabled students of all abilities and talents to bridge the gap between their academic classroom experiences and the application of these skills in the workplace. The ten-week project culminated in student presentations and portfolios, and the completed student-designed and engineered "Genetic Robotics" were displayed to involve the entire student body, other faculty, parents, and members of the educational community. The aim of our integrated unit was to provide all of our students with access to experiences that allowed them to go beyond isolated facts to put issues in context.

FUTURE IMPLEMENTATION OF GENETIC ROBOTICS

The teachers benefited from the exchange of ideas with their colleagues, the group dynamics of designing and implementing an interdisciplinary unit, and the enthusiasm and energy of their students. Also, they agreed with many of today's influential education reformers knowledgeable in the area of integrated curriculum: secondary teachers should be generalists first and specialists second. They plan to elaborate on this project and implement it again in the future. They will have an excellent opportunity to include language arts teachers, mathematics teachers, sociology teachers, foreign language teachers, or lifestyles teachers in their curricular plan. The expertise and knowledge these teachers have gained will contribute greatly to future units and will help students make cross-curricular connections to the theme of "pioneering" and increase the relevance of the material to the world outside the classroom.

STUDENT PORTFOLIOS

The ongoing assessment of our students was recorded in a three-ringed notebook portfolio that included everything subject to evaluative criteria, and demonstrated the higher-order thinking skills our students will need to live in a complex world. We told them to think of the portfolio as a paper trail, showing where they have traveled intellectually.

Student portfolios contained journal entries, library research papers on famous geneticists such as Gregor Mendel and famous sculptors such as Nam June Paik, reaction papers to the field trip and guest speaker, decision matrices, newspaper clippings of Dolly-the-sheep cloning articles, sketches of the phenotypical robot prototypes, teacher-made handouts, Punnett squares illustrating probability results, science and art lecture notes, pamphlets and brochures picked up on the field trip, and in some cases, email correspondence. The portfolio also contained student self-assessment and a place for the parents/guardians and the teachers to record comments, interpretations, and judgments. These materials were collected in collaboration with the students and teachers, and showcased and celebrated the achievement of each student.

The students helped formulate the evaluative criteria and assess their own progress on "talk back" evaluation sheets; in this way, they became shareholders in their own learning. In addition, resourcefulness, problem solving, communication, group interaction, flexibility, and innovativeness were encouraged. Finally, the voice of students' perceptions, in the form of postproject student "talk back" reaction papers, was an important diagnostic tool to determine the effectiveness of the interdisciplinary project in order to make modifications for future lessons.

THE SCIENCE IN "GENETIC ROBOTICS"

Many textbooks oversimplify the nature of gene action. By asking students to assume the role of creator of a three-dimensional "human" robot sculpture, we helped them understand the difference between genotype and phenotype, dominance and recessiveness, the difference between probability and inevitability, and the importance of genetics in determining health. For those students who have difficulties with formal reasoning, physical models can be important tools for assessment.

The real-life story of Dolly the sheep, where Scottish scientists revealed they used a mammary cell from an adult ewe to create Dolly in the exact genetic image of her mother (Crenson 1997) happened about two weeks into the implementation of the "Genetic Robotics" project. Cloning can contribute to the diagnosis and curing of genetic diseases, and the groundbreaking development of the sheep clone served to substantiate the curricular unit as usable by teachers to enhance the critical problem-solving abilities and the ethical sensibilities of students in solving molecular biological problems.

THE ART IN "GENETIC ROBOTICS"

In addition to helping our students create an authentic assessment of ongoing portfolio development, we facilitated student discovery of understanding how to create three-dimensional sculptures based on human phenotype characteristics. As our students inquired into the rules that govern the passage of genetic information from one generation to the next, they translated the genotypes (for example, genetic makeup such as XX or XY) by producing three-dimensional, human-like robots using found objects and art supplies to visually demonstrate the phenotypes (for example, physical characteristics such as hair color or eye shape) of the DNA.

CONCLUSION

The major contributions of an integrated science and art curriculum to the study of education are in revealing misconceptions regarding the relationships between the arts and sciences. Within an interpretive framework, an art and biology integrated unit of study has tremendous potential for determining the perceptions of students toward biological ethical issues, art's place in the curriculum, and the value of an integrated curriculum.

CHAPTER 5

Two Selected Integrated Activities for Secondary Students

What on earth is creativity? How can a concept be so important in human thinking, so crucial to human history, so dearly valued by nearly everyone yet be so elusive?

—Betty Edwards, *Drawing on the Artist Within*

In this chapter, the fine points of two selected integrated activities for secondary students are detailed and include:

- Pop-up Greeting Cards Inquiry: an integrated secondary unit connecting mathematics (geometry), visual art (graphic design), and language arts (poetry, library research, and reaction papers)
- Genetic Robotics Inquiry: an integrated secondary unit connecting science (biology), visual art (sculpture), and language arts (library research and journaling)

These projects are classroom tested and geared to high school-level students. They are presented with the criteria necessary to encourage students to use their unique abilities to define their own problem, determine a solution for that problem, and construct a working model of their solution.

Specifically, these curricular approaches offer the following extrinsic advantages:

1. Students hone communication skills through contact with representatives from area businesses.
2. Teachers who may be unfamiliar with the integrated approach at the secondary level are not only provided with a step-by-step

template for success but gain valuable methodological and pedagogical insights.
3. Parents and teachers witness firsthand the finished products high
school students are capable of producing when challenged and
motivated in this way.

The artistic, mathematical, literary, and scientific content of the projects included here are intrinsically important because the relevance of
making connections that resemble the world outside the classroom enables students to build the essential characteristics of a productive citizen in the twenty-first century. In each case, parents and guardians are
considered "partners" in the education process and should be invited
and encouraged to attend curriculum planning sessions, classes, field
trips, guest lectures, celebrations, and final presentations.

POP-UP GREETING CARDS INQUIRY

An Integrated Secondary Unit Connecting Mathematics (Geometry), Visual Art (Graphic Design), and Language Arts (Poetry, Library Research, and Reaction Papers)

Unit Overview

This project is designed to enhance higher levels of thinking through
creative problem-solving activities that involve the integration of visual
art and geometry with students of all abilities. This unit includes a wide
variety of multisensory activities involving the basic elements of art
and principles of design, in conjunction with geometric theorems about
parallel, perpendicular, and intersecting lines and planes.

"Pop-up Greeting Cards Inquiry" will take about five weeks to complete in twenty-five class sessions of fifty-five-minute blocks or about
three weeks to complete in fifteen class sessions of ninety-minute
blocks. This unit is planned for a team-taught class of forty-five students but would be suitable for a class of any size. Since most classrooms contain students with diverse abilities and backgrounds, this unit
is sensitive to that fact. Only minor accommodations will be necessary
for students with special needs.

There are several cooperative group activities that assume the students have had prior experience working effectively in cooperative
groups. If students have not had prior experience working effectively in

Integrated math and
art classroom
students construct
pop-up greeting
cards

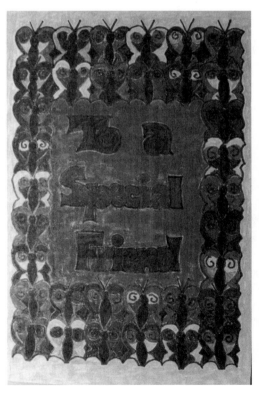

Tessellation pop-up greeting
card project

According to the National Science Teaching Association,
physical models can be important tools

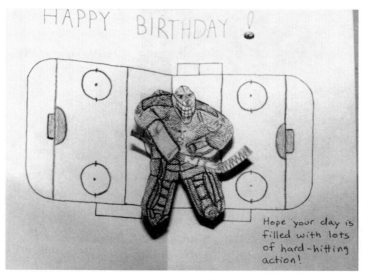

Pop-up greeting card sample

cooperative groups, then these lessons should be preceded by a discussion of the expected behaviors and responsibilities when working cooperatively with others. Further, it is recommended that students be in teams of four or five at the start of the unit, as this facilitates easy transition into group work and allows for a team-based behavior management system if desired.

To support this unit, an arranged environment should be created in the classroom that can include posters, artifacts, pop-up greeting card samples, trade and resource books, and tessellation illustrations. Bulletin boards should be created using students' ongoing and finished works. When this project was implemented at a high school in Cincinnati, Ohio, the Gibson Greeting Card Company, an internationally known American greeting card manufacturer, lent valuable support by becoming involved in the education of the students. For example, card designers volunteered their time to "evaluate" students' pop-up greeting cards at the end of the project. Applications of geometry and art outside of the classroom were supported by a field trip to the Gibson Greeting Card Company, which was designed to familiarize the students with the work of graphic designers and other artists in the greeting card industry. Executives of the company paid for a chartered bus for the students to visit the plant, where each student received a gift package. Moreover, while at the site, in addition to learning about potential career opportunities, the students toured the departments of projection printing, die cutting, and creative graphic design. Students wrote reaction papers of their experience at Gibson Greetings and these journal entries were included in the students' final portfolios.

Purpose of the Unit

The purpose of the "Pop-up Greeting Card Inquiry" integrated curriculum is to recognize individual difference in students while providing the conditions and experiences by which all students can become mathematically literate in geometry and visually literate in graphic design, and experience a sanctuary for individual expression and creativity.

Budget for the Unit

After applying for a Martha Holden Jennings Foundation Grant, the Cincinnati teaching team was awarded funds to implement this unit.

The budget, which was based on forty-five students, included:

- Professional release time for teacher planning $ 300
- Three-ring binders with tabs (for student portfolios)   300
- Necessary supplies
  Ellison machine and special die-cut tools   1,000
  Card stock and tracing paper   300
  Office supplies (postage, workshop handouts)   200
  Art supplies (markers, pens, paints, cutting knives, blades,
  cutting mats, drafting supplies, etc.)   400
  Books and resource materials   300
- Necessary travel, accommodations, reservations
  Local travel to companies involved in project   200
- Other   500
  Prizes for students
  Celebration parties for students
- Total $3,500

Goals and Objectives of the Unit

This unit is designed to:

1. reveal how subjects of art (graphic design) and math (geometry) are mutually reinforcing;
2. integrate the philosophy of teamwork;
3. break down the barriers that separate the two subjects of mathematics and art;
4. facilitate student understanding of how to create three-dimensional pop-up greeting cards.

This unit is designed to enable students of all abilities and talents to:

1. explore paper-engineering concepts though a hands-on approach to discovery learning and realistically simulate the die-cutting and graphic design methods used by greeting card manufacturers;
2. bridge the gap between their academic classroom experiences and the application of these skills in the workplace;
3. identify a hypothesis of the mathematics involved in creating their own pop-up card design, then test it by making a prototype of their card design using X-acto knives and drafting tools;

4. increase spatial visualization skills by investigating the art elements of line, shape, color, and value, and several principles of design, including balance, proportion, and rhythm;
5. replicate the design techniques used by graphic designers;
6. write reaction papers;
7. conduct library research involving the work of M.C. Escher;
8. compose poetry that is congruent with their card design;
9. investigate tessellation patterns, symmetrical patterns, transformational geometric designs, and Mendelbrot fractals.

Unit Assessment

There are three components for assessment of student learning:

1. Portfolios—They are designed to demonstrate the higher-order thinking skills that students need to live in a complex world. Students are to think of their portfolio as a "paper trail" showing where they travel intellectually.
   The students' portfolios are an ongoing assessment recorded in a three-ringed notebook, including the following elements that are subject to evaluative criteria:
   • Journal entries (three journal prompts total)
   • Field trip reaction paper
   • Mathematical calculations (tessellation designs)
   • Sketches (of ideas for greeting cards)
   • Poetry (compositions designed to coordinate with the card's theme)
   • Library research (historical and contextual information on M. C. Escher)
   • Presentation notes and ideas
   • Market research (graphs, surveys, etc.)
2. Unit test and quizzes—The students are quizzed on course definitions and concepts as they apply the mathematics involved in their finished pop-up greeting cards and M. C. Escher's tessellation art.
3. Finished pop-up greeting cards—The finished cards are self-evaluated as well as being evaluated by the students' peers and by employees of the Gibson Greeting Card Company, as well as the teachers per prior product specifications and guidelines.

Week 1: Pop-up Greeting Cards, Library Research and Presentations on M. C. Escher and Graphic Design

Objectives

Students of all abilities and talents will:

1. engage in library research to familiarize themselves and the class with the work of artist M. C. Escher;
2. participate in cooperative learning groups;
3. prepare a presentation and present their findings as a group to the class;
4. prepare a finished, typed research report of their findings.

Materials Needed

Books, Websites, magazines, and other resources that:

1. illustrate M. C. Escher's works;
2. discuss the cultural influences on M. C. Escher (geometric Islamic designs);
3. demonstrate other artists and graphic designers who were influenced by Escher;
4. portray biographical information of M. C. Escher;
5. illustrate graphic design concepts (that is, contemporary and historical greeting card design).

Anticipatory Set

Today, we are beginning an exciting unit on the work of Dutch graphic design artist Mauritius Cornelius Escher (1898–1972), who created many perplexing tessellations. Throughout the unit, we will participate in a wide variety of activities and will have many opportunities to work in cooperative groups on special presentations and projects. Today, we are going to form groups for our library research on M. C. Escher and graphic design that will be in place for the remainder of the unit.

Procedures

1. Put students in teams of four or five students per team.
2. Assign each team a topic to research from the following:
   • Classical works of M. C. Escher
   • Biography of M. C. Escher

- Influences on M. C. Escher
- Contemporary artists influenced by M. C. Escher
- A day in the life of a contemporary graphic designer

3. Student teams create presentations that will be performed in front of the class on the third day. This may be done in the form of a play, a newscast, report, discussion, and so forth.
4. After each presentation, team members will prepare an outline for the class on their topic.
5. The presenters will respond to questions as the class takes notes on the information presented.
6. After the presentations, the students will evaluate their own listening behavior using an assigned student-generated rubric.

Closure

- What is something interesting that you learned today that you didn't know before?
- Did your group have any problems while researching information or putting together your presentations?
- Discuss cooperation when working in groups and the importance of giving each member of the group a chance to contribute ideas.

Evaluation

- Group presentations will be teacher-evaluated as to content.
- Students will self-assess their listening behavior using an assigned student-generated rubric.

Week 2: Pop-up Greeting Cards, Overview of Tessellation Techniques

Objectives

Students of all abilities and talents will:

1. discuss and analyze M. C. Escher's work *Reptiles*
2. create the following:
   - modified polygons by translation
   - modified parallelogram by translation
   - modified hexagon by translation
3. investigate Mendelbrot fractals

Materials for Teacher

Resource Books:

- Britton, J., and W. Britton. 1992. *Teaching Tessellating Art: Activities and Transparency Masters.* Palo Alto, CA: Dale Seymour Publications.
- Seymour, D., and J. Britton. 1989. *Introduction to Tessellations.* Palo Alto, CA: Dale Seymour Publications.

Visuals:

- *Reptiles* by M. C. Escher (copyright 1990 M. C. Escher Heirs/Cordon Art, Baarn, Holland). Image may be an overhead, slide, poster, postcards, or book illustration.
- Overheads of plane tessellating grids

Materials for Students

- Isometric dot paper
- Tracing paper
- Pencil
- Straight edge
- Eraser

Anticipatory Set

This week we are continuing our exciting unit on the work of artist M. C. Escher and his geometrically designed tessellations. (Show illustration of *Reptiles*.) Dutch graphic design artist Mauritius Cornelius Escher (1898–1972) created many perplexing tessellations. His preoccupation with tessellations developed after a 1936 visit to the Alhambra in Granada, Spain, an old Moorish palace decorated with Islamic mosaics in geometric patterns. Unlike the Moors, Escher did not restrict himself to abstract geometrical designs. Instead, he drew animated forms like the lizard we see in *Reptiles*, crawling out of Escher's two-dimensional sketch to explore the "real" world before rejoining his fellow reptiles in the interlocking design.

Procedures:

1. Show visuals of M. C. Escher's *Reptiles*.

2. Show overheads of examples of plane tessellating grids and explain the following: Escher's designs were plane tessellations. We define a tessellation of the plane as a pattern of shapes that fills the plane without any gaps or overlaps. The basis for any tessellating pattern is a grid of polygons—triangles, quadrilaterals, or hexagons. Any triangle or quadrilateral will tessellate the plane. In addition, any hexagon whose opposite sides are parallel and congruent will tessellate. Various techniques can be used to form triangles, quadrilaterals, or hexagons into animate shapes that tessellate the plane. These techniques involve transformations that we call translation, rotation, and reflection.

3. Pass out the isometric dot paper to students.

4. Teachers illustrate the following translations using an overhead projector and isometric dot paper (please see Britton and Britton 1992 for instructions):
   - Modifying Polygons by Translation. In this case, the tessellation design is to modify two sides of a polygon and translate those modifications to the opposite sides. A translation of a shape is a slide of that shape without rotation.
   - Modifying Parallelogram by Translation. In this case, the tessellation design is to modify two sides of a parallelogram and translate those modifications to the opposite sides.
   - Modifying Hexagons by Translation. We can extend this method to include regular hexagons or, more generally, any hexagon having parallel and congruent sides. In hexagonal tessellations, we have three sets of opposite sides to be modified.

5. Students practice creating all three types of tessellations.

6. Teachers monitor student progress and assist where necessary.

Closure

- What is something interesting that you learned today that you didn't know before?
- Did you have any problems while creating your tessellations?

Evaluation

- Students will self-assess their tessellations using the assigned rubric.
- Students will present their final tessellation designs to the class, who will engage in a formal critique of their artwork.

Weeks 3–6: Pop-up Greeting Cards,
Overview of Die-cutting Techniques

Objectives

Students of all abilities and talents will:

- work in their assigned groups to survey a population (over e-mail, in person, or by telephone);
- work in groups to chart and graph their survey data;
- individually compose a poem or verse to accentuate their card's theme;
- individually create a "prototype" of their finished greeting card;
- work in groups and use the Ellison machine and special die-cut tools to create pop-up greeting cards based on their individual handmade "prototype";
- work in groups to investigate potential career opportunities in mathematics and visual art through the design, production, and sale of student-designed greeting cards.

Materials

- Ellison machine and special die-cut tools
- Card stock paper
- Tracing paper
- Markers, paints, pens,
- Art cutting knives and blades
- Cutting mats
- Drafting supplies

Anticipatory Set

Over the next two weeks, we will learn how to design and manufacture pop-up greeting cards comparable to the ones you find in the store. Instead of simply memorizing from the textbook, you are going to have the opportunity to actually apply the geometric principles and artistic techniques you have been learning to transform your two-dimensional drawings to three-dimensional space.

Procedures

1. Teachers review tessellation design with students (please see Britton and Britton 1992).

2. Teachers and students examine professionally manufactured pop-up greeting cards.
3. Teachers demonstrate die-cutting techniques.
4. Students create a pop-up greeting card prototype that integrates their tessellation design.
5. As students finish final card prototypes, teachers demonstrate use of the Ellison machine and die-cutting techniques.
6. Teachers monitor student progress and assist where necessary.

Closure

- What is something interesting that you learned today that you didn't know before?
- Did you have any problems while creating your tessellations?
- Did you have any problems with the die-cutting techniques?

Evaluation

- Students will self-assess their greeting cards using an assigned student-generated rubric.

GENETIC ROBOTICS INQUIRY

An Integrated Secondary Unit Connecting Science (Biology), Visual Art (3-D Found Object Sculpture), and Language Arts (Library Research and Journals)

Unit Overview

In "Genetic Robotics Inquiry," students explore the chromosome theory of heredity through a hands-on approach to discovery learning. Specifically, they study the rules that govern the passage of genetic information from one generation to the next, and then translate the genetic codes (DNA) of the chromosomes they "inherit" by making a prototype of a "human" three-dimensional robot using found objects and art supplies. Resourcefulness, problem solving, communication, group interaction, flexibility, and innovativeness are encouraged and valued in the "Genetic Robotics Inquiry." According to the National Science Teaching Association (NSTA), "For students who have difficulty with formal reasoning, physical models can be important tools for assessment" (1996, 9).

Many textbooks oversimplify the nature of gene action. By asking students to assume the role of creator of a three-dimensional "human" robot sculpture, the teaching team enables them to understand the difference between genotype and phenotype, dominance and recessiveness, the difference between probability and inevitability, and the importance of genetics in determining health.

Scottish scientists revealed that they used a mammary cell from an adult ewe to create Little Dolly in the exact genetic image of her ovine mother. This "real-life" documentary of science fiction is useful to substantiate the curricular unit since cloning can contribute to the diagnosis and curing of genetic diseases. The groundbreaking story also enhances students' critical problem-solving abilities by increasing awareness of the ethical sensibilities and issues involved in solving molecular biological problems.

Student discovery of understanding how to create three-dimensional sculptures based on human phenotype characteristics is also facilitated. As the students inquire into the rules that govern the passage of genetic information from one generation to the next, they translate the genotypes (that is, the DNA or genetic makeup) by producing three-dimensional, human-like robots using found objects and art supplies to visually demonstrate the phenotypes (that is, physical characteristics of the DNA).

Time Frame

"Genetic Robotics Inquiry" takes approximately ten to twelve weeks to complete in fifty to sixty class sessions of fifty-five-minute blocks or about seven to nine weeks to complete in thirty-five to forty-five class sessions of ninety-minute blocks. This unit is planned for a team-taught class of forty-five students but would be suitable for a class of any size. Since most classrooms contain students with diverse abilities and backgrounds, this unit is sensitive to that fact. Only minor accommodations will be necessary for students with special needs.

Two cooperative group activities assume the students have had prior experience working effectively in cooperative groups. If students have not had prior experience working effectively in cooperative groups, then these lessons should be preceded by a discussion of the expected behaviors and responsibilities when working cooperatively with others.

Integrated classroom with multi-age grouping

Problem-based learning helped students connect the biology and art

Student robot constructions cul-
minate in final presentations

Student "Genetic Robotic" sculpture

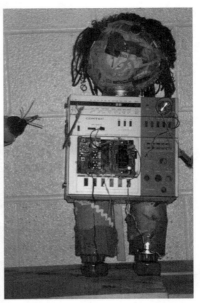

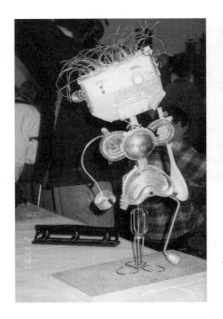

Student genetic robots constructed
from found objects

Ample storage space to accommodate the students' sculptures is required for this project. Therefore, to support this unit, an arranged environment should be created in a large classroom and include:

- shelving for the students' sculptures
- shelving for the students' tool kits
- shelving for the students' portfolios
- posters and bulletin boards
- sculpture samples
- reference books and materials

When this unit was implemented in a high school in Cincinnati, Ohio, a biology teacher's ninth-grade honors class was combined with an art teacher's multigrade-level and multiability-level students in the art room because that classroom was large enough to accommodate forty-five students, each of whom constructed a large robot from found objects.

Applications of science and art outside of the classroom were supported by field trips designed to familiarize the students with the work of molecular geneticist Tom Doetschman at the University of Cincinnati Medical Center and the work of sculptor Nam June Paik at the Michael Solway Gallery, the Cincinnati Art Museum, and the Contemporary Art Center. Dr. Doetschman, who uses advanced genetic technology to breed special strains of mice for medical research, gave a presentation to the students in the state-of-the-art lecture room at the center and then took them on a guided tour of the laboratories. Students also visited one of the studios of Nam June Paik, an internationally known Fluxus artist whose work incorporates video technology and sculpture. Students witnessed firsthand the construction involved in Paik's finished works. Michael Solway, the gallery owner, gave the students a personalized tour of the facility and discussed the work of Paik with them.

At the Cincinnati Art Museum, the students had the opportunity to view Paik's masterpiece, *Powell Crosley Jr.*, a sculpture based on the historical memorabilia of radio and television pioneer, inventor, engineer, scientist, and native Cincinnatian Powell Crosley Jr. At the Contemporary Art Center, they viewed *Metrobot*, a monumental outdoor public robotic sculpture equipped with a digital display designed to advertise exhibits at the CAC. A visiting local artist and sculptor, Fred Ellenberger, spoke to the students about the relationships between science and art. He explained the basic principles involved in constructing sculptures and the necessity of incorporating the talents of a variety of scientific engineers, including mechanics, designers, physicists, and technicians.

Early in the project, parents and guardians should be invited to attend any curriculum planning sessions, classes, field trips, guest lectures, celebrations, and final presentations. For this unit, sculptures are constructed from found objects that parents and guardians can help collect. Parents may also wish to volunteer to assist in the more complex assemblages.

The project culminates with student presentations of the finished robot sculptures and the robot "offspring" sculptures. Students discuss the rationale for their robots' outward characteristics (phenotypes) and their Punnett square calculations (genotypes). They also justify why they choose to use particular materials to construct their robots. For example, if the robot "inherited" the gene for blue eyes from its parents, then a student might discuss the probability of blue eyes and materials such as blue flashcubes that would represent the blue eyes on the robot. Parents/guardians and the student body should be invited to the final presentations, which might be followed by a pizza party (that is, a celebration).

The finished robot sculptures are displayed in the school library along with the students' portfolios for the entire student body and for school personnel to experience. Moreover, the local newspaper provides a forum for students to demonstrate their inquiry and to provide the community with news of the ongoing integrated unit.

A teaching team that strives to provide a nonthreatening environment will enable students the opportunity to freely generate and synthesize ideas that are new for them. Portfolio development, robot development, presentations, and library research, rather than standardized examinations, should provide the basis for assessment. Finally, students' voices and perceptions, in the form of pre- and post-"talk back" reaction papers, serve as an important tool for the teaching team to determine the effectiveness of the project in order to make modifications for future integrated curricular units.

Purpose of the Unit

The fundamental purpose of the "Genetic Robotics Inquiry" is to recognize individual differences in students while providing the conditions and experiences by which all students become scientifically literate in genetics, visually literate in 3-D sculpture, and providing a sanctuary for individual expression and creativity.

Theme of the Unit

In "Genetic Robotics Inquiry," the strengths of the disciplines of art and of biology are kept intact while providing a connection between the two diverse fields. The theme of "pioneers," resulting from the teaching team's clustering and reclustering of a semantic web as they planned the integrated unit of study, guides the unit. (Nam June Paik is a pioneer in the field of video technology and inventor of the "jump cut" as seen on Music Television (MTV), and Gregor Mendel was a pioneer in the field of genetics with his pea pod experiments.)

Budget for the Unit

The school's Ohio Venture Capital Grant awarded funds to the Cincinnati teachers to implement this unit. The budget, which was based on forty-five students, included the following:

- Professional release time for teacher planning $ 300
- Three-ring binders with tabs (for student portfolios) 300
- Necessary supplies
  - Individual tool kits 1,000
  - Paper 300
  - Office supplies (postage, workshop handouts) 200
  - Art supplies (glue guns, markers, pens, paints, cutting knives, blades, cutting mats, drafting supplies, etc.) 400
  - Books and resource materials 300
- Necessary travel, accommodations, reservations 200
  - Local travel to institutions involved in project
- Other 500
  - Prizes for students
  - Celebration parties for students
  TOTAL $ 3,500

Goals and Objectives of the Unit

This unit is designed to:

1. reveal how the two subjects of biology (genetics) and visual art (3-D found-object sculpture) are mutually reinforcing;
2. integrate the philosophy of teamwork;
3. break down the barriers that separate the subjects of science, language arts, and art;
4. facilitate student understanding of how to translate DNA (dominance and recessivness in gene inheritance) to create found-object humanoid sculptures;
5. provide all students with access to experiences that will allow them to go beyond isolated facts to put issues in context.

This unit is designed to enable students of all abilities and talents to:

1. explore 3-D sculpture techniques and concepts and the chromosome theory of heredity through a hands-on approach to discovery learning;
2. study the rules that govern the passage of genetic information from one generation to the next;
3. translate the genetic codes (DNA) of the chromosomes they "inherit" by making a prototype of a "humanoid" three-dimensional robot using found objects and art supplies;
4. bridge the gap between their academic classroom experiences and the application of these skills in the workplace;
5. write reaction papers;
6. conduct library research involving the history of genetic research and geneticists and the history of sculpture and artists;
7. investigate Punnett square calculations.

Unit Assessment

When this unit was implemented in a suburban high school in Cincinnati, Ohio, the interdisciplinary classroom became a site for authentic assessment. The view of the learner who constructs meaning and advocates using "real-life" problems with more than one right answer was promoted. Therefore, evaluations were based on alternative assessment strategies rather than on standardized examinations, be-

cause the teaching team's primary purpose was to determine competence rather than mere acquisition.

The final evaluation rubric is based on disciplined artistic and scientific inquiry and reflects the kinds of mastery demonstrated by experts
in the fields of art and science who create knowledge. Students are encouraged to perform as scientists, writers, historians, and artists. The
teaching team should enable students to integrate their knowledge by
pulling together their learning rather than displaying bits and pieces
separately. In order to do this, teachers emphasize in-depth knowledge
of genetics and sculpture rather than mere surface facts. There are two
components for assessment of student learning:

1. Portfolios—The portfolios are designed to showcase and cele-
   brate the achievements of each student and demonstrate the types
   of higher-order thinking skills that students increasingly need to
   live in a complex world. Students, teachers, and parents/
   guardians are to think of the student portfolio as a "paper trail"
   showing where each student travels intellectually. The following
   portfolio items are an ongoing assessment recorded in a three-
   ringed notebook:
   • Journal entries (for example, ethics of Dolly the sheep clone,
     cloning humans, genetically engineered foods, etc.)
   • Newspaper, Website, and magazine clippings (for example,
     Dolly the sheep and other genetically engineered phenomenon
     in the news)
   • Library research papers (for example, famous creative geneti-
     cists such as Gregor Mendel, Francis Crick, James Watson, and
     Rosalind Franklin, or other artists who incorporate technology
     and science into their art, such as Nam June Paik)
   • Lecture notes (for example, biology and art history)
   • Biology vocabulary and definitions
   • Sculpture vocabulary and definitions
   • Punnett square calculations (for example, illustrations of prob-
     ability results)
   • Graphs and charts of the statistical analysis of the Punnett squares
   • Sketches of the phenotypic robot prototypes
   • Essay detailing the specifics of their robot designs
   • Teacher-made handouts
   • Artifacts (for example, pamphlets and brochures from field
     trips, e-mail correspondence)

- Reaction papers (for example, to the field trips and guest speakers)
- Self-assessment (for example, platform statements of students on performance and learning)
- Talk backs (for example, a place for students, parents/guardians, and teachers to record comments, interpretations, and judgments)

2. Finished genetic robotic sculptures—Student discovery of understanding how to create three-dimensional sculptures based on human phenotype characteristics is the second component for assessment of student learning. As the students inquire into the rules that govern the passage of genetic information from one generation to the next, they translate the genotypes by producing three-dimensional, human-like robots using found objects and art supplies to visually demonstrate the phenotypes. The finished sculptures are self-evaluated as well as being evaluated by the students' peers and also by the teachers per prior product specifications and guidelines.

Weeks 1 and 2: Genetic Robotics Inquiry, Introduction, Field Trips, and Guest Speaker

The following schedule is based on ten to twelve weeks of fifty-five-minute, team-taught integrated classes.

Weekly Objectives

Students of all abilities and talents will:

1. view a presentation of Gregor Mendel's theories of genetic inheritance;
2. view a presentation of Nam June Paik's 3-D media sculptures;
3. brainstorm portfolio contents and materials that will be subject to evaluative criteria;
4. visit a genetics lab at a local medical center;
5. visit an art gallery featuring 3-D works;
6. brainstorm questions for visiting artist;
7. collect found objects for sculptures (for example, old radio chassis, wood, plastics, yarn, buttons, etc.).

Materials

- Forty-five three-ring binders (2" wide) and dividers with tabs
- Overheads of types of sculpture
- Overheads of biology concepts relating to genetics

Books, Websites, magazines, posters, and other resources that:

- illustrate the work of Nam June Paik
- illustrate the work of Gregor Mendel
- discuss the cultural influences on Nam June Paik
- demonstrate other artists and graphic designers who were influenced by Nam June Paik
- demonstrate other geneticists who were influenced by Gregor Mendel
- portray biographical information of Nam June Paik
- portray biographical information of Gregor Mendel
- illustrate 3-D sculpture concepts
- illustrate DNA model

Anticipatory Set

Does anyone remember the announcement that Scottish embryologists had succeeded in cloning a sheep from a single cell? The debate over future human cloning will be one of the things we discuss this quarter as we begin our integrated biology and art unit. Throughout the unit, we will participate in a wide variety of activities, including making a 3-D robot sculpture, and we will also have many opportunities to work in cooperative groups on special presentations and projects. Today, we are going to brainstorm together contents for your final portfolios and a rubric for the final evaluation of your projects.

Procedures

1. Project introduction
2. Art slide presentation: "Types of Sculpture"
3. Distribution of portfolios and dividers
4. Biology presentation: "Mendel's Theories"
5. Pass out permission slips for field trips
6. Brainstorm assessment rubric and portfolio contents

7. Brainstorm questions for visiting artist
8. Biology presentation: "Sex-linked Traits"
9. Art presentation: "The Sculpture of Nam June Paik"
10. Field trip to the medical center (genetics lab)
11. Field trip to the art gallery or museum (with examples of Paik's work, if possible)
12. Introduction to library research papers for next week

Journal Prompt

- Talk about something interesting that you learned this week that you didn't know before.

Periodic Assessment

- Students will self-assess their listening behavior using an assigned student-generated rubric.

Week 3: Genetic Robotics Inquiry, Library Research

Weekly Objectives

Students of all abilities and talents will:

1. engage in library research to familiarize themselves and the class with the work of Fluxus artist Nam June Paik and other artists whom he influenced and who influenced him;
2. engage in library research to familiarize themselves with the work of Gregor Mendel and other geneticists who have built on his work with the pea pod experiments;
3. participate in cooperative learning groups;
4. prepare a presentation and present their findings as a group to the class;
5. prepare a finished typed research report of their findings;
6. continue to collect found objects for robot sculptures.

Materials

Resource and reference books, magazines, and Websites on:

- biology
- genetics

- science history
- history of art
- Fluxus art
- sculpture

Visuals of:

- The work of Nam June Paik, Pablo Picasso, Louise Nevelson, Mark Di Suervo, Claes Oldenburg, Marisol Escobar, and Duane Hanson (that is, artists who incorporate science and art)
- *Powell Crosley Jr.* sculpture by Nam June Paik
- Gregor Mendel, Walter Sutton, Thomas Hunt Morgan, Rosalind Franklin, Maurice Wilkins, James Watson, and Francis Crick (that is, genetic scientists who creatively worked toward significant biological discoveries)
- DNA double helix

Anticipatory Set

This week we are continuing our exciting unit on the work of artist Nam June Paik and his robotic sculptures, and historical geneticist Gregor Mendel. Nam June Paik is a pioneer in the field of video technology and inventor of the "jump cut" as seen on Music Television (MTV) videos; Gregor Mendel was a pioneer in the field of genetics with his pea pod experiments. Both people are at once "creative" and "technical." When might artists need to be "technical" and/or "analytical" and when might scientists need to be "creative"?

Procedures

1. Put students in teams of three or four per team for library research.
2. Assign each team a topic from Part I: The Scientists and Part II: The Artists (below).

Part I. The Scientists:
Choose from the following list of scientists and their contributions to the field of genetics and include the following:

- definitions of the key words associated with each scientist
- contributions of each scientist to the idea that DNA carries genetic code

- the time period in which he or she was working
- the specific experimentation for which the scientist is known
- how each scientist built on the work of genetic pioneer Gregor Mendel
- any special "imaginative" or "creative" activities the scientist might have engaged in to do her or his work
  A. Gregor Mendel
     Key Words:
     a. experiments
     b. dominant
     c. recessive
     d. factors (genes)
     e. pea pods
  B. Walter Sutton
     Key Words:
     a. microscope
     b. gene location
     c. chromosome theory of heredity (genes are located on chromosomes)
  C. Thomas Hunt Morgan
     Key Words:
     a. experiments with tiny fruit flies (*Drosophilia*)
     b. linkage groups
     c. sex-linked genes
     d. polygenic traits (height, body weight, skin color)
  D. James Watson and Francis Crick
     Key Words:
     a. DNA (nucleic acid)
     b. RNA (ribonucleic acid)
     c. proteins (amino acids)
     d. experiments with how DNA could copy itself (replicate)
     e. DNA Structure or Model (double helix/spiral/linked strands of nucleotides)
     f. nucleotides (molecules or units that make up the DNA polymer)
     g. creation of the Helical Theory
     h. Nobel Prize
  E. Rosalind Franklin and Maurice Wilkins
     Key Words:
     a. feminist issues (What struggles did [do] intelligent women face in the scientific world? For example, why was Franklin

not given formal recognition for her part in the discovery of the DNA double helix model?)

b. three-dimensional form of DNA

c. sugar phosphate

d. crystallographer

e. X-ray diffraction

f. X-ray photography

g. polypeptide chains

Part II. The Artists:

Choose from the following list of artists and their contributions to the field of sculpture and include the following:

- definitions of the key words associated with each artist
- materials her or his sculptures are made from
- any special "technical" or "scientific" expertise and or support the artist may have needed to create her or his artwork
- the art movement(s) with which the artist's sculpture is associated
- the artists' inspirations
  A. Pablo Picasso
     Key Words:
     a. pioneered the use of found objects as objects of art
     b. juxtaposition
     c. planes
     Suggested Artworks:
     a. *Woman's Head* (Cor-ten Steel—Richard J. Daley Center, Chicago, IL)
     b. *Head of a Bull* (Leather and metal bicycle saddle and handlebars)
  B. Louise Nevelson
     Key Words:
     a. ready-made wooden shapes
     b. assemblage
     c. repeat pattern
     d. monochromatic
     e. geometric (shapes that are based on the laws of geometry)
     f. organic (shapes that are naturalistic and lifelike)
     Suggested Artworks:
     a. *Nightscape III* (Cincinnati Art Museum)
     b. *Sky Landscape III* (Cincinnati Public Library)

C. Nam June Paik
  Key Words:
  a. technology
  b. video sculptures
  c. video as an artistic medium
  d. Korean-American
  e. Fluxus art
  f. laser discs
  Suggested Artworks:
  a. *Metrobot* (Contemporary Art Center)
  b. *Powell Crosley Jr.* (Cincinnati Art Museum)
D. Mark Di Suervo
  Key Words:
  a. linear constructivist/minimalist
  b. balance/scale/proportion
  c. space and environmental setting
  Suggested Art Work:
  a. *Atman* (Art Academy of Cincinnati)
E. Claes Oldenburg
  Key Words:
  a. pop artist
  b. engineering
  c. monumental
  d. everyday objects
  Suggested Artworks:
  a. *Batcolumn* (20 tons of aluminum, Sears Tower,
     Chicago, IL)
  b. *Falling Shoestring Potatoes* (painted canvas)
  c. *Giant Ice Bag* (plastic and metal)
F. Marisol Escobar
  Key Words:
  a. pop artist
  b. bright colors
  c. surface texture
  d. realism
  e. abstract
  Suggested Artworks:
  a. *Woman and Dog* (wood, plaster, synthetic polymer, Whitney
     Museum, New York)
  b. *The Royal Family*

G. Duane Hanson

Key Words:

a. photo-realistic sculpture

b. lifelike

c. life-size

d. wax museum

e. 3-D illusion

Suggested Artworks:

a. *Couple with Shopping Bags* (polyvinyl, fiberglass)

b. *Tourists* (wigs, glasses, jewelry)

3. Student teams create presentations and outline handouts for the other students based on their research.

4. After each presentation (which may be done in the form of a play, a newscast, report, discussion, and so forth), team members prepare an outline for the class on their topic.

5. The presenters will respond to questions as the class takes notes on the information presented.

6. After the presentations, the students will evaluate their own listening behavior using a student-generated rubric.

Journal Prompts

• Discuss something interesting that you learned this week that you didn't know before.

• Discuss any problems you may have had while writing your papers and preparing your presentations

Periodic Assessment

• Students will self-assess their reports and presentations and the presentations of their peers using an agreed-upon student-generated rubric.

Weeks 3 and 4: Genetic Robotics Inquiry, Punnett Square Calculations and Robot One Design

Weekly Objectives

Students of all abilities and talents will:

• calculate monohybrid Punnett squares

• roll dice to determine "phenotypes" (see the genetic trait checklist)

- begin sketches of Robot One based on the phenotypes they "inherit"
- begin Robot One construction

Materials

- Genetic trait checklist
- Dice
- Paper
- Markers
- Pencils
- Found objects

Anticipatory Set

By now, you have probably discovered that artists generally have an idea or an inspiration before they construct their sculptures. Your inspiration for your robot sculpture is the idea that DNA carries the genetic code. You will use the "genotypes" (a specific inherited gene) to illustrate the "phenotypes" (hair color, hair texture, eye color, eye shape, etc.) using found objects. Your robot may be abstract or it may be realistic. Think of the artists that you researched (or that the students in class presented to you) and describe what you like about their sculpture techniques. What ideas did they have that may have inspired you? What sort of craftsmanship did they use that inspired you?

Procedures

1. Biology Presentations:
   Monohybrid cross and Punnett squares
   Dihybrid cross and Punnett squares
2. Using the genetic trait checklist, students roll a die to determine whether the thirty-four genotypes on the checklist are (1) homozygous dominant, (2) heterozygous, or (3) homozygous recessive. For example, the feature "hair" on the genetic trait checklist has three genotypes: (1) texture, (2) widow's peak, and (3) color. Let's take color as an example, and let's say that:
   Black is homozygous dominant.
   Brown is heterozygous.
   Blonde is homozygous recessive.

If a student rolls:

a 1 or a 2 = homozygous dominant

a 3 or a 4 = heterozygous

a 5 or a 6 = homozygous recessive

The student then records the information on the genetic trait checklist, which will serve in the Punnett square calculations.

3. The following are features, with the genotypes in parentheses, which appear on the student's genetic trait checklist.

At least eighteen "genotypes" should be shown as "phenotypes" on the students' robots (either abstractly or realistically, depending on the student's personal artistic sculpture style):

- Eyes (spacing, position, size, color, eyelashes, eyebrow shape, and eyebrow position)
- Face (shape, chin)
- Hands (finger length, bent little finger, hitchhikers thumb)
- Hair (texture, widow's peak, color)
- Nose (size, nostrils, shape)
- Mouth (size, shape of lips, dimples)
- Ears
- Torso
- Legs
- Feet
- Sex
- Sex-linked trait

4. Students define the following vocabulary:

- Heredity
- Inheritance
- Hybrid gene pair
- Pure gene pair
- Alleles
- Dominant
- Recessive
- Phenotype
- Genotype
- Homozygous
- Heterozygous
- Independent assortment
- Segregation
- Punnett square
- Probability

- Chromosome
- Linked genes
- Sex chromosomes
- Sex-linked trait
- Autosomes
- Mutation
- Chromosomal mutation
- Nondisjunction
- Gene mutations
- Frameshift mutations
- Incomplete dominance
- Codominance
- Polygenic
- Selective Breeding
- Inbreeding
- Hybridization
- Mutagens
- Human genome
- Karyotype
- Pedigree
- Crossing over

5. Art Presentations
   Construction of sculpture using found objects
   Class critique of student sketches thus far
6. Students start cross-genetic for Robot One.

Journal Prompts

- After reading the Dolly-the-Sheep article, comment on any aspect of cloning that interests you.

Periodic Assessment

- Students will self-assess their surveys using an assigned student-generated rubric.

CHAPTER 6

Where Do We Go from Here?

There is a need for a new vision of preparing students to see patterns and connections among the different facts they learn. The pervasive notion that the organizational structure of a subject-centered school day with six or seven periods is the only way to successfully educate students is at odds with revealing to the students that learning is a lifelong journey of making meaningful connections and that schooling is a process. There is a need for students to develop higher-order thinking skills and to take responsibility for constructing meaning for themselves.

Integrated curriculum not only helps learners perceive connections but also promotes a sense of connectedness and the habit of lifelong learning, which are essential components of a truly educated person. In the interest of striving to create a better world, schooling must include the ongoing growth and reflection of students and teachers in a continuous search to better understand that learning is constant and connected.

The necessary role for citizens of the twenty-first century is one of synthesizer and creative problem solver. Although problems are often associated with the development and implementation of integrated curricula at the high school level, I believe that the problems are outweighed by the intellectual growth for both students and instructors. Like all models in education, teaming art and science curriculum and teaming art and math has both strengths and weaknesses. After designing and implementing integrated units of study that include science, math, art, and language arts at the high school level, I have concluded that a well-planned and carefully executed integrated curriculum benefits both teachers and students. It is clear to me that practitioners seeking to improve ways of revealing the world to students should choose the path of integration as a means of creating a learner-centered classroom where both children and adults pursue useful knowledge.

Efforts to bring about change such as this must be collaborative and inclusive. Included in the search for better schooling must be the voices of the students and teachers involved in the process of change as they learn how to understand their purpose within an integrated epistemological framework of inquiry. As curriculum developers gain an understanding of how this can be better facilitated, the task of designing and implementing integrated curriculum should become easier. In my view, the only way to improve thematic integrated units at the secondary level is to seek the point of view of the students and teachers involved: try it, ask questions, listen to the voices of the participants, evaluate it, change it to make it better, try it again. The result, though still not perfect, will probably be better than comparable approaches done without adequate effects, repeated testing, refinement, and most importantly, without the expression of authentic voices.

References

Armstrong, T. 2000. *Multiple intelligences in the classroom*. Alexandria, VA: Association for Supervision and Curriculum Development.

Beane, J. A. 1991. The middle school: The natural home of integrated curriculum. *Educational Leadership* 49(2):9–13.

———. 1993. Problems and possibilities for an integrative curriculum. *Middle School Journal* 25(1):18–23.

———. 1995. Curriculum integration and the disciplines of knowledge. *Phi Delta Kappan* 76:616–622.

Boyer, E. L. 1983. *High school: A report on secondary education in America*. New York: Harper & Row.

———. 1990. *Scholarship reconsidered: Priorities of the professoriate*. Princeton, NJ: The Carnegie Foundation for the Advancement of Teaching.

———. 1995a. *The basic school: A community for learning*. Princeton, NJ: The Carnegie Foundation for the Advancement of Teaching.

———. 1995b. The educated person. In *Toward a coherent curriculum*, edited by J. A. Beane, 16–25. Alexandria, VA: Association for Supervision and Curriculum Development.

Boyer, E. L., and A. Levine. 1981. *A quest for common learning: The aims of general education*. Washington, DC: The Carnegie Foundation for the Advancement of Teaching.

Bredeson, P. V. 1992. Responses to restructuring and empowerment initiatives: A study of teachers' and principals' perceptions of organizational leadership, decision making, and climate. Paper presented at the meeting of the American Educational Research Association, April, San Francisco, CA.

Brooks, J. G., and M. G. Brooks. 1993. *In search of understanding: The case for constructivist classrooms*. Alexandria, VA: Association for Supervision and Curriculum Development.

Brown, J. Carter. 1993. Excellence and the problem of visual literacy. *Design for Arts in Education* 84(November/December):3.

Clark, E.T. 1997. *Designing and Implementing an Integrated Curriculum: A Student-Centered Approach.* Brandon, VT: Holistic Education Press.

Crenson, M. 1997. Geneticists raise flock of questions. *Cincinnati Enquirer,* 25 February.

Deutschman, A. 1992. Why kids should learn about work. *Fortune* (August).

Dewey, J. 1915. *Schools of tomorrow.* New York: Free Press.

——— . 1916. *Democracy and education.* New York: Macmillan.

——— . 1934. *Art As experience.* New York: Perigee Books.

——— . 1938. *Experience and education.* New York: Macmillan.

Drake, S. M. 1990. The monomyth brings meaning to change. *Canadian School Executive* 10:15–18.

——— . 1991a. The journey of the learner: Personal and universal story. *The Educational Forum* 56(1):47–59.

——— . 1991b. How our team dissolved the boundaries. *Educational Leadership* 49(2):20–22.

——— . 1993. *Planning integrated curriculum.* Alexandria, VA: Association for Supervision and Curriculum Development.

Drake, S. M., J. Bebbington, S. Laksman, P. Mackie, N. Maynes, and L. Wayne. 1992. *Developing an integrated curriculum using the story model.* Toronto: O.I.S.E. Press.

Edwards, B. 1979. *Drawing on the right side of the brain: A course in enhancing creativity and artistic confidence.* Los Angeles: Houghton Mifflin.

——— . 1986. *Drawing on the artist within: A guide to innovation, invention, imagination, and creativity.* New York: Simon and Schuster.

Eisner, E. 1972. *Educating artistic vision.* New York: Macmillan.

——— . 1988. *The role of discipline-based art education in America's schools.* Los Angeles: The Getty Center for Education in the Arts.

——— . 1991. *The enlightened eye: Qualitative inquiry and the enhancement of educational practice.* Upper Saddle River, NJ: Prentice Hall.

——— . 1992a. The federal reform of schools: Looking for the silver bullet. *NAEA Advisory.* Reston, VA: National Art Education Association.

——— . 1992b. A slice of advice. *Educational Researcher* 21(5):29–30.

——— . 1994. *The educational imagination: On the design and evaluation of school programs.* New York: Macmillan.

——— , ed. 1978. *Reading, the arts, and the creation of meaning.* Reston, VA: National Art Education Association.

Erickson, H. L. 1995. *Stirring the head, heart, and soul.* Thousand Oaks, CA: Corwin.

Fogarty, R. 1991. Ten ways to integrate curriculum. *Educational Leadership* 42(October):61–65.

Fowler, C. B. 1994. Strong arts, strong schools. *Educational Leadership* 52: 4–9.

Freire, P. 1983. The importance of the act of reading L. Slover. *Journal of Education* 165:(winter)5–11.

Fullan, M. 1993. *Change forces: Probing the depths of educational reform.* London: Falmer Press.

—— . 1999. *Change forces: The sequel.* London: Falmer Press.

Fullan, M., and A. Hargreaves. 1991. *What's worth fighting for in your school?* Toronto, Ontario: Ontario Public School Teachers' Federation.

Gardner, H. 1980. *Artful scribbles.* New York: Basic Books.

—— . 1982. *Art, mind, and brain.* New York: Basic Books.

—— . 1983a. *The unschooled mind: How children think and how schools should teach.* New York: Basic Books.

—— . 1983b. *Frames of mind: The theory of multiple intelligences.* New York: Basic Books.

—— . 1988. Creativity: An interdisciplinary perspective. *Creativity Research Journal,* 8–26.

—— . 1990. *Art education and human development.* Los Angeles: The Getty Center for Education in the Arts.

—— . 1993a. *Multiple intelligences: The theory into practice.* New York: Basic Books.

—— . 1993b. *Creating minds: An anatomy of creativity seen through the lives of Freud, Einstein, Picasso, Stravinsky, Eliot, Graham, and Gandhi.* New York: Basic Books.

Gardner, H., and Y. Dudai. 1985. Biology and giftedness. *Items Social Science Research Council* 35:1-6.

Gaur, A. 1984. *A history of writing.* London: The British Museum.

Goals 2000: Educate America Act. U.S. Public Law 103-227. 103rd Cong., 2nd sess., 31 March 1994.

Goodman, K. 1986. *Language learning.* New York: Routledge.

Hall, G. E., and S. F. Loucks. 1978. A developmental model for determining whether the treatment is actually implemented. *American Educational Research Journal* 14(3):263–276.

—— . 1981. Program definition and adaptation. *Journal of Research and Development in Education* 14(2):46–58.

—— . 1982. Bridging the gap: Policy research rooted in practice. In Part 1 of *Policy making in education: Eighty-first yearbook of the national society of the study of education,* edited by A. Lieberman and M. McLoughlin, 133–158. Chicago, IL: University of Chicago Press.

Hall, G. E., R. C. Wallace, and W. A. Dosset. 1973. *A developmental conceptualization of the adoption process with educational institutions.* Austin, TX: University of Texas.

Hausman, J. 1994. *National standards for visual arts education.* Reston, VA: National Art Education Association.

Heck, S., S. M. Stiegelbauer, G. E. Hall, and S. F. Loucks. 1981. *Measuring innovation configurations: Procedures and applications.* Austin, TX: University of Texas.

Henri, R. 1923. *The art spirit.* Philadelphia: J. B. Lippincott.

Hurd, P. 1991. Why we must transform science education. *Educational Leadership* 49(October):33–35.

Jacobs, H. H., ed. 1989. *Interdisciplinary curriculum: Design and implementation*. Alexandria, VA: Association for Supervision and Curriculum Development.

—————. 1991. The integrated curriculum. *Instructor*, 22–23.

Jacobs, H. H., J. Hannah, W. Manfredonia, J. Percivalle, and J. Gilbert. 1989. *The interdisciplinary model: A step-by-step approach for developing integrated units of study*. Alexandria, VA: Association for Supervision and Curriculum Development.

Johnson, J., S. Farkas, and A. Bers. 1997. *Getting by: What American teenagers really think about their school*. A Report from Public Agenda.

Kellough, R. 1996. *Integrating language arts and social studies for intermediate and middle school students*. Englewood Cliffs, NJ: Prentice Hall.

Lazear, D. 1991. *Seven ways of knowing: Teaching for the multiple intelligences*. Pallantine, IL: Skylight.

—————. 1992. *Teaching for multiple intelligences: Fastback 342*. Bloomington, IN: Phi Delta Kappa Educational Foundation.

—————. 2000. *The intelligent curriculum: Using MI to develop your students' full potential*. Tucson, AZ: Zephyr Press.

Loucks, S. F., B. W. Newlove, and G. E. Hall. 1975. *Measuring levels of use of the innovation: A manual for trainers, interviewers, and raters*. Austin, TX: University of Texas.

Lounsbury, J. H., ed. 1992. *Connecting the curriculum through interdisciplinary instruction*. Columbus, OH: National Middle School Association.

Lowenfeld, V. 1947. *Creative and mental growth*. New York: Macmillian.

Martinello, M., and G. Cook. 2000. *Interdisciplinary inquiry in teaching and learning*. Upper Saddle River, NJ: Prentice Hall.

McFee, J. 1970. *Preparation for art*. San Francisco: Wadsworth.

Miller, J. 1988. *The holistic curriculum*. Toronto: O.I.S.E. Press.

National Science Foundation. 1995. Bringing the arts into the sciences. *Summary of awards: Instructional materials development, fiscal years 1991–1994*. Washington, DC: National Science Foundation.

National standards for arts education: What every young American should know and be able to do in the arts. 1994. Reston, VA: Music Educators National Conference.

Osborne, B. 1993. Understanding change in a time of change. Paper presented at the Annual Conference on Creating the Quality School, March, at Oklahoma City, OK.

Page, J. A, and F. M. Page Jr. 1994. The teacher's role in restructuring: The power of one—a case study. Paper presented at the meeting of the American Educational Research Association, April, New Orleans, LA.

Pate, P. E., E. R. Homestead, and K. L. McGinnis. 1993. Designing rubrics for authentic assessment. *Middle School Journal* 25(2):25–27.

——. 1997. *Making integrated curriculum work: Teachers, students, and the quest for coherent curriculum.* New York: Teachers College Press.

Patterson, J. L. 1993. *Leadership for tomorrow's schools.* Alexandria, VA: Association for Supervision and Curriculum Development.

Pestalozzi, H. 1951. *The education of man,* translated by H. Norden and R. Norden. 1894. Reprint, New York: Philosophical Society.

Piaget, J. 1972. *The epistemology of interdisciplinary relationships.* Paris: Organization for Economic Cooperation and Development.

Reich, R. 1992. *The wealth of nations.* New York: Vintage Books.

Schramm, S. L. 2000. Genetic Robotics: An Integrated Art and Biology Curriculum. *Art Education Journal* 53(3):40-45.

Schramm, S. L. 1999a. Intellectual tension: Connecting biology and visual art in the secondary curriculum. *American Secondary Education* 27:3–16.

——. 1999b. Related webs of meaning between the disciplines: Perceptions of high school students who experienced an integrated curriculum. *Ohio Art Education Journal* 37:18–40.

——. 1999c. The role of the arts in national education: An opportunity and a challenge. *Teacher Education Journal of South Carolina* 8:48–49.

Sizer, T. R. 1984. *Horace's compromise: The dilemma of the American high school.* Boston: Houghton Mifflin.

——. 1992. *Horace's school: Redesigning the American high school.* Boston: Houghton Mifflin.

——. 1996. *Horace's hope: What works for the American high school.* Boston: Houghton Mifflin.

Stoehr, J., and S. Buckey. 1997. *Getting started: Projects for the integrated curriculum.* Tucson, AZ: Zephyr Press.

Tchudi, S., and S. Lafer. 1996. *The interdisciplinary teacher's handbook: Integrated teaching across the curriculum.* Portsmouth, NH: Boynton/Cook.

U.S. Department of Education. 1983. *A nation at risk: The imperative for educational reform.* Washington, DC: U.S. Department of Education.

——. 1991. *America 2000: An education strategy sourcebook.* Washington, DC: U.S. Department of Education.

——. 2001. *No child left behind.* Washington, DC: U.S. Department of Education.

Viadero, D. 1993. Students fall short on "extended" math questions, analysis finds. *Education Week* 15(7):16.

About the Author

Susan L. Schramm is an assistant professor of Curriculum Studies at the University of South Carolina, with research and teaching emphases in integrated arts-based curriculum, cultural studies, and women's studies. Her research appears in *Art Education Journal, International Journal of Educational Research, Journal of Communications and Minority Issues*, and numerous other publications. She received her Ph.D. in Educational Administration (Curriculum Studies) at Miami University.